AUTHENTIC MEXICAN
COOKING

AUTHENTIC MEXICAN
COOKING

80 DELICIOUS, TRADITIONAL RECIPES FOR TACOS, BURRITOS, TAMALES, AND MUCH MORE

Scott Myers and Gabriele Gugetzer
Photography by Ulrike Schmid & Sabine Mader
Illustrations by Olaf Hajek
Translated by Victoria Yam

SKYHORSE PUBLISHING

CONTENTS

PREFACE

FROM MEXICO. WITH LOVE.

Some experiences from our youth affect us so deeply that they stay with us for a lifetime. They are ones that we try to recall, see, feel, and hear decades later. My first trip to Mexico was such an experience. It was the summer of 1967, and I was seven years old. With my Mexican stepfather, I drove in a VW bug from Los Angeles to the south of Mexico. As we crossed the border, the changes could not have been more noticeable. The relative order and security of my own land was replaced with a true explosion of life. After we had traveled through the dry, northern desert regions for a few days and had driven by the snow-covered mountainsides of Mother Sierra in central Mexico, we passed fruitful land with corn fields as far as the eye could see. Our goal, however, was *Teotihacan*, as it was called by the Aztecs, later translated by the Spanish conquistadors as *La Ciudad de los Dióses*, City of the Gods. Today, this place is called Mexico City and is composed of the largest and most concentrated congregation of people in the world.

I spent the next month with my Mexican family. They gave me a nickname (Mexicans like to do this a lot): *el guerito*, "small blond boy." Apart from that, they treated me like a Mexican, took me in with open arms, and showed me the whole wonder of my newly adopted country. I have the liveliest memories of the glorious days I spent in the kitchen with my grandmother and aunts. I helped them with the preparation of *salsas, moles, enchilades, tamales, sopas, chile rellenos, chilaquiles*, and a dozen other dishes, learned the recipes that had been taught to them by countless generations of women, and gained insight into their secret knowledge of food, life, and love. In Mexico, these three topics simply cannot be separated from one another. And so began my lifelong love story with this country, its people, its art, its music, and above all else, its cuisine, which belongs to the oldest, most complex, and most diverse country in the world.

About forty years later, I went on another unbelievable trip. I moved from California to Bavaria with my German wife, Heike, and three young children, Charlotte, Isabella, and Lukas. I had one goal: to bring Germans closer to the miracle of authentic Mexican cuisine. I was convinced that authentic cuisines from the different regions of Mexico, which were always fresh and hand-prepared, would be a huge success in Germany, and the name of our restaurant, we agreed, was to be *Milagros* (Miracle).

Mexico is equally heart-wrenchingly beautiful and heart-wrenchingly sad. The Mexicans admire their author and philosopher Octavio Paz, who invented the famous phrase *La Raza Cósmica*, the "funny race," for the Mexicans of today. According to Paz, they are a mix of Mesoamerican rites and customs of a century-old Spanish tradition with a healthy dose of the twenty-first century lifestyle. It is an honor for me to present this book–*La Raza Cósmica*–to you lovely readers.

Un Abrazo Fuerte
Scott Myers

MEXICAN CULINARY MIRACLE
THE MILAGROS RESTAURANT

David Sterling

With my help, Scott Myers, the owner and the soul of this modern restaurant, Milagros, intended to bring the magic of Mexican cuisine to Germany. He comes from California. I am actually a New Yorker. So both of us are non-Mexicans. And of all things, we decided to open an authentic Mexican restaurant in the heart of Munich? This would be a particularly exceptional challenge, that much was true.

When Scott asked me to help him with his plans for this venture, I was immediately excited and extremely determined to support him with intense vigor. He wanted to export the authentic flavor, the sun and happiness, the "spirit" of his beloved Mexico to the passers-by of the snow-covered Alps—and admittedly, without wanting to risk a huge loss. A terrific idea! At least in theory. But how can this practically operate in a city that otherwise is only familiar with mediocre restaurants? We will probably need a miracle, I thought, and somehow, I got the Spanish word for miracle, *milagros*, stuck in my head. The perfect name for our purposes and the restaurant!

The first step was deciding on the look and design of the restaurant. To do this, I had to design a kitchen and a menu with at least eighty authentic Mexican dishes. The cooks needed to be trained and the dishes had to be genuine and authentically Mexican. A truly Herculean task, and I thank God that I did not have to stand alone as Scott and his wonderful team always stood by my side.

MILAGROS
Frauenstraße 9
(the Viktualienmarkt)
80469 Munich, Germany
www.milagros-restaurant.de

I needed a real miracle: the right ingredients and the right coworkers. Without authentic ingredients, the food would not taste Mexican. And without cooks who knew the flavors of Mexico, it also would not have worked. Four young cooks from Mexico were brought over right before the opening to share their knowledge with our Munich colleagues, kind of like a cultural exchange. Then Richie Wee took over as the head chef and shared how authentic and real this cuisine tasted with our junior chefs.

We found a lot of our ingredients directly outside our front door at the day food market, one of the biggest, most beautiful, and surely the most abundant in all of Germany. It had almost everything we needed for our menu: vanilla beans, real cocoa beans, aromatic pineapples, a variety of chilies, old tomato varieties, and ripe avocados. Good quality has its price, but only really good products lead to a great flavor experience. This cookbook is an expression of passion and love—for Mexican cuisine, the country of Mexico, and its people. We, with our outside perspective, were more and more astonished every day by this culture. Mexican cuisine always became new and surprising and, in the best way, exotic for us Americans. With this cookbook, you can now cook truly genuine, pure Mexican cuisine at home with these recipes. And if you really want to experience it at the highest level, then you should visit Scott and his team in Milagros in Munich. And maybe Scott, the Milagros restaurant, the miracle, and I can inspire you with our love and passion. At any rate, that would be my great wish.

To the miracle!
David Sterling, Mérida, Yucatán, México

David Sterling was born in Oklahoma City. He studied design and cooking at the University of Michigan and then went to New York, where he lived and worked for the next twenty-five years. In the year 2003, he moved to Mérida, the capital of the Mexican federal state of Yucatán. On this peninsula, he opened *Los Dos*, the only culinary school in the country dedicated to genuine Yucatán cuisine. Find more information located at: www. los-dos.com

THE WONDERFUL MEXICAN KITCHEN

THE CULINARY MEXICAN INFLUENCE
The Origins of Fusion Cooking

Mexico has influenced the European kitchen for a very long time. Everything began with the command of Spanish King Ferdinand, who in the year 1511 instructed his *conquistadores* to bring aboard ten turkeys to Spain on the way back from Mexico. The birds were so popular in Europe that this Mexican souvenir quickly ousted the pheasant as the favorite bird in banquets. Since the mid-sixteenth century, tomatoes, which Christopher Columbus brought with him from Mexico in 1493, have been grown in the Mediterranean. And how crazy the royal families were for chocolate during the Baroque period—only as a drink, chocolate bars were still unknown—everyone knows that.

It is not at all surprising that so many products originate in Mexico. With 761,606 square miles, Mexico features many different climates and landscapes: deserts in the northern part of the country, mountains all around Mexico City in central Mexico, tropical rainforests in Chiapas, wetlands in the south in the Tabasco region. Historians believe that since 1492, numerous Mexican markets opened due to this diversity. When these products came to Europe, it must have been unbelievably exciting. A Neapolitan cookbook from the year 1692 consists of, for example, a recipe for tomato sauce. Today, one can no longer imagine Italian cuisine without tomatoes. In the eighteenth century, a clever French chocolate maker filed down the chocolate until he had invented the chocolate bon-bon.

It wasn't a new phenomenon for different cultures to blend in the kitchen. The famous *mole poblano* sauce is comprised of Mexican chocolate and chili peppers, yet equally as important are Asian spices

and raisins, almonds, and sesame seeds, which the Spaniards introduced to the New World. "Creole" is what one calls this fusion of Mexican and European cuisine. It still exists today, just like the kitchens of dozens of Native American tribes, who, to this day, still live in Mexico.

Mexican cuisine is steadily developing and is constantly changing. Enrique Olvera from the world-known restaurant *Pujol* in Mexico City cooks in such an innovative, ingenious, and contemporary fashion that one could well describe his cooking as "New Mexican." In the whole English-speaking sphere, professionals and amateurs alike have fallen in love with Mexican cuisine, and the cookbooks by Diana Kennedy and Rick Bayless have sold millions of copies. It is no wonder that the Mexican cuisine of UNESCO has been recognized as a World Cultural Heritage site.

BETWEEN THE CARIBBEAN AND THE PACIFIC
The Regional Cuisines of Mexico

Mexico is a huge country with bone-dry deserts and snow-covered mountain ranges. The cuisine is, however, the most sustainable in these coined desert regions. Between the Pacific and the Caribbean, 6,170 miles of desert stretch from the Gulf of Mexico to the Gulf of California. The unbelievable abundance of fish and seafood stems from the extensive bodies of water, whose use was developed during the centuries of the New and Old worlds. Regionally, there are many different recipes: *Ceviche* with citrus aromas from Nayarit, *Huachinango*, or white fish in a rich sauce from Veracruz, prawns in a coat of coconut from Campeche . . . These are only a few examples of the many dishes from the regional cuisines of Mexico, which we have jotted down for you.

CHILI PEPPERS
The Fiery Mexican Soul

Christopher Columbus brought back many things from his trip to the New World that Europeans had never seen before: potatoes, corn, cocoa beans, and, naturally, chili peppers. There are over two hundred kinds of chili peppers, and more than one hundred of these are indigenous to Mexico. Thus, a very exceptional skill developed when dealing with chili peppers in the Mexican kitchen. They are healthy and produce color, aroma, flavor—and spiciness. Yet spiciness is actually more of a secondary trait. Good Mexican cuisine uses substantially less spices than, say, what we are familiar with at Tex-Mex restaurants or from the Thai kitchen. If you are unsure about the flavoring, simply start with a small dose. You can always make a dish more spicy. Removing spiciness is more difficult (i.e., with potatoes or with diluting a dish).

Ancho: **A good four inches long and fairly broad. Red-brown. Somewhat fruity in flavor, sweeter than all other dried chilies. When fresh (and green), these are called Poblanos.**

Arból: **Around three and a half inches long, red, slender, and curved. Spicy—comparable with cayenne pepper.**

Chipotle: **Not a type, but rather, a smoked Jalapeño chili pepper. Dark-brown with a smoked aroma that, afterwards, smells sweet. Also produced in canned goods (Chipotle en adobo).**

Guajillo: **Is medium length and slender with a pointed end. Used when dried and is very spicy.**

Habanero: **Small and is very dainty looking—like a lantern. Between an orange and green color, independent from the level of ripeness. Blazing hot.**

Mulato: **At least four inches long and rather narrow. Has a smoky flavor.**

Pasilla: **A good eight inches long, rather narrow, aromatic, and medium spicy. Dark brown in color.**

Serrano: **Around one and a half inches long. Green and fades to red and yellow. Often pickled in oil or can be bought in a can. Can be used when fresh or when dried. Spicy.**

TEQUILA
Spirit of the Gods

Tequila is one of the most misunderstood alcoholic drinks on the face of this planet. Very few people outside of Mexico have drank genuine, real, authentic tequila. When correctly manufactured, tequila is produced from the root of the agave plant and from nothing else. This one hundred percent agave tequila differentiates itself in high quality and is considerably more flavorful than those that are mass produced and made with sugar, flavor strengthener, and preservatives.

There are really only three authentic types of tequila: silver, reposado, and anejo. The silver gets its name from its clear appearance. It does not age in oak barrels like the others, rather, it is drinkable immediately after distillation. A good silver should have a smooth-tasting finish. The reposado is aged in an oak barrel for anywhere between six and nine months. Then it acquires a golden color, is smooth in the finish, and tastes sweet and tangy on the tongue. The anejo is stored in a barrel for one to two years and should be drunk like a good whiskey or cognac. Anejos are unbelievably smooth in the finish and have a huge, flavorful complexity—tangy, herbal, and sometimes reminiscent of honey.

Whoever drinks good tequila can attest that he is revitalized through the enjoyment of it, the spirit of the gods. Because only tequila is manufactured from a plant, which can first only be harvested after twenty years, the Mexican sun and earth has been carrying a true spirit of the gods for decades!

CHOCOLATE
The Drink of Kings

Like all Aztec rulers before him, King Moctezuma lived and feasted famously—he was the undisputed God-King of Mexico—and in a befitting manner. Every day, his staff prepared around three hundred dishes, reserved only for him. The leftover budget was used towards another thousand dishes. At the end of every meal, the God-King expressed his power with a ritual: he drank hot chocolate, because at the time, cocoa beans were considered the gold of the Aztecs and a symbol for power and wealth. Pulverized, dissolved in hot water, sweetened with honey, and beaten until frothy, this gold of the Aztec subjects became the drink of kings.

LONG LIVE THE WOMAN!
Powerful Women in the Kitchen

It probably seems contradictory that a feminist movement developed from the calculated place of the kitchen in an otherwise completely male-dominated culture. Yet women still did not have much of a say in anything, so the kitchen was their kingdom—here, they enforced their rules; here, they could exchange ideas with each other. When important topics had to be discussed, even if only about the academic achievement of their children or questions about the political situation, the women went to the kitchen to discuss such topics.

A figurehead of the women's movement "from the kitchen," was the mystic, poet, and nun, Sor Juana Inés de la Cruz. She lived in the seventeenth century, but was ahead of the times in all sorts of things. For instance, she masterfully connected potential "unwomanly" topics with cooking. "I could tell you all something about the secrets of nature, which I discovered with cooking," she wrote, and then went on about the laws of chemistry. She is famous for her quote, "If Aristotle had cooked, then he would have written a whole lot more!" Unfortunately, it was unavoidable that the writings of Sor Juana vom Bischof von Puebla were censored as "scientific research that cannot be taken with a straight face." At the end of the nineteenth century, there was an initial increase of cookbooks about authentic Mexican dishes, such as *tamales* or *chiles en nogada*, within the market; these were symbolic for the growing Mexican self-awareness during the times of revolution. Authentic recipes served as a declaration of war on the political caste of men in the country—and to say that cooking would be a bore!

BITTERSWEET
Sex in the Kitchen

The conquering of Mexico and the subsequent authority of the Catholic Church did not change the basic daily life of Mexicans, but new standards and rules—how one should properly and morally live, think, and feel—developed. The emotional and sexual freedoms of the Mexican tribes were sinful in the eyes of the Catholic Church and were rigorously suppressed.

However, it is truly surprising that within these tribes, which already were the first to have given up on the custom of human sacrifice, primal needs were the only ones that were difficult to get rid of, especially since the Spanish conquerors really did not provide any good role models, and the advantage of their powers were sometimes quite brutally exploited.

Mexicans like to think that cooking and eating is an important channel of emotions. The successful novel, *Like Water for Chocolate* by Laura Esquivel, is a wonderful and lively exaggeration of this idea. The hero of the novel, Tita, is not allowed to marry the love of her life, Pedro, because she must fulfill her duty as the youngest daughter and take care of her widowed mother. To be at least near Tita, Pedro decides to marry her older sister. A hot-blooded chef, Tita unleashes her feelings in the kitchen, and with her food, everyone experiences what she feels. Her dishes make people break out in tears, or experience sexual ecstasy. Poor Pedro must experience how much Tita is suffering through his own body. At least his own suffering is sweetened through the costly creations of his beloved Tita. Her passion for Pedro burns so hot, she literally burns the house to the ground. Chilies are not the only thing that are hot and spicy in the Mexican kitchen!

BROWNING VEGETABLES

In the Mexican kitchen, tomatoes, chili peppers, and garlic are frequently browned. In this process, no fat or grease is used, and the browning is also not a fermenting process, but rather, its purpose is to provide more flavor and color. Therefore, it is important that with garlic, one does not use too much heat. Garlic that is burned tastes bitter and can ruin an entire dish. So here it goes:

Take the washed tomato and brown both sides for a few minutes on medium heat until it turns a really dark color, but is not yet burned, nor has it gone soft. The tomato should still be firm on the inside. If the tomato browns longer than this, it will cook through and become soft; and it won't be easy to scrape out the seeds. [Photos 1+2]

Garlic should be browned in the husk because it protects it from burning. For best results, imagine that the garlic is milk. It will bubble over and burn if no one is watching ... [Photo 3]

Chili peppers should also not be burned, otherwise, they will have a bitter and sour aftertaste. Pack browned chili peppers in a plastic bag and leave them to sweat for ten minutes. Then let the skin peel back lightly on its own. [Photo 4]

1

2

3

4

PREPARING CHILIES

Kitchen gloves and chili peppers belong together. If you have ever forgotten that you had peeled chilies, and ten minutes later, accidentally touched your eyes (with really hot chilies, it is enough to just let them touch the skin), then you know the reason for this. It burns like hell.

1. Up to eighty percent of the spiciness of chili peppers is hidden within the seeds and the white membrane. If one likes the aroma of the chili, but not the spiciness or cannot tolerate it, then one can adjust the level of spiciness by removing both of these.

2. As a rule of thumb: the smaller the chili pepper, the spicier it is. Slice the chili lengthwise, then from the stalk, pry open and fold back. Leave only the seeds, and with a spoon, scrape out the white membrane.

3. Also, if chili peppers are browned, this does not mean that any of the spiciness has been taken away during the process. The same goes for freezing chili peppers. Even after this, they are still as spicy as they were when you first got them. At least your active ingredient, Capsaicin, is used in pepper spray. Thus you should always work with kitchen gloves and afterwards, you should also clean your cutting board with hot water and dish soap, while wearing your kitchen gloves.

4. The smaller the chili, the finer it should be cut, since this then distributes its spiciness equally throughout the dish.

HOW TO HANDLE THE SPICINESS OF CHILIES

The browning and subsequent soaking of chilies is an alternative method to get rid of their spiciness. They also come in many different types of flavors: fruity, chocolaty, peppery . . . always choose fresh chilies with smooth, solid surfaces.

1. Toast the chilies in a pan at mid-temperature until they show color and develop an aroma. If you sniff them, they will smell spicy.

2. Place the toasted chilies in a heat-resistant bowl and fill with hot water. Let them steep until the water cools down to a lukewarm temperature.

3. The soaked chilies will only be squeezed through a strainer. This works best with a wooden spoon. Use a fine-mesh strainer so that the seeds stay within the strainer. Squeeze well so that you may extract as much pulp as possible.

4. Simmer the chili pulp in a pan with some type of grease. This will change the color and darken them. The aroma is intense, but it is no longer as spicy as it was before.

THE PERFECT GUACAMOLE

Guacamole is a dip, a sauce, a topping, and a side dish, and there is really no one who does not like it. What are important for a delicious guacamole are, above all other things, avocados. There are almost five hundred different kinds of avocados, and some are not even as big as an apricot; there are some that are round, pear-shaped, and elongated. In this part of the world, the dark, nubby Hass avocado came out on top—and for good reason, since its flavor is very aromatic.

1. A couple of ingredients always belong in a guacamole: besides avocados, you will need chilies, lime juice, and salt. Finely minced tomatoes, cilantro, or scallions also match very well with guacamole.

2. One does not achieve the best consistency with a food processor or with a blender. The guacamole will then become too smooth, and every additional ingredient will also become too runny. For the best results (and most typical, at that), guacamole should be mashed in a large mortar with a pestle.

3. The pestle from the mortar prevents the unattractive discoloration of the guacamole. You can also quietly prepare this dip in advance. Remove the pestle, but only right before serving. The pestle tip goes for all dishes involving avocados.

4. As long as no oxygen comes in contact with the guacamole, it retains its appetizing green color. Thus you must press kitchen wrap directly on top of the guacamole's surface, so that it clings tightly, and do not stretch the kitchen wrap over it, since this will collect oxygen underneath the guacamole, and the appetizing light-green will turn into a gray-brown sludge.

JACK-OF-ALL-TRADES TORTILLAS

Tortillas are unbelievably diverse. They can be served on their own, tightly rolled, loosely rolled, or stacked on top of each other. Traditionally, the tortilla is made from cornmeal. Wheat flour was first brought to the country by European conquerors. From then on, wheat farming was funded because with this flour, hosts would bake for the Catholic supper.

1. So here is the easiest way: Open cornmeal tortillas are served with diverse side dishes. You can then roll them together yourself. These small cornmeal tortillas are called **tacos** and are served in special concession stands, otherwise known as "taquerias."

2. A tortilla made from wheat flour that contains a saturated filling, which is also served rolled, is known as a **burrito**. Breakfast burritos with egg, meat, pickled onions, and guacamole are terrific!

3. Wheat flour tortillas that are filled with cheese and then baked until the cheese melts are called **quesadillas**. Before serving, they are divided into triangles and can be eaten with your hands.

4. Cornmeal tortillas that are quickly fried in hot grease, then dried, stacked on top of one another, and divided into six parts are called "tortilla chips," which are also known as **totopos**.

1

2

3

4

1

2

3

4

TAMALES - THE SUPREME DISCIPLINE

Tamales were only made for festivities because they were really elaborate to prepare. One could also say that Mexicans make a party out of the preparation of tamales, in which friends and family participate. You can find a recipe for the filling on page 125.

1. Tamales are steamed in a dried corn husk. Of course this also works with aluminum foil, and similarly, like with cooking in a banana leaf, the aroma carries over into the filling. It has a fine, smoky flavor.

2. Corn has quite a number of different colors, from white, over to a mellow yellow, even to a light-blue.

3. Take a soaked corn husk in your hand, thinly brush the rims with filling, and then spoon some more in the middle. Do not overfill because the filling will rise during steaming. Place the sides loosely on top of one another and fold over the ends.

4. Seal the tamales with some kitchen yarn or with a strip of corn husk. The seal must be so tight that the tamal (this is the singular form) does not open, but also not so tight that there is still room for the rising filling when steaming.

REFRESHERS!

Drinks and Cocktails

AGUA FRESCA DE LIMÓN Y MENTA
LIME-MINT DRINK

Limes have a distinctive flavor, and with their refreshing, lightly bitter aroma, they are typical in the Mexican kitchen. Their juice freezes well.

PRODUCES ABOUT 6⅓ CUPS (1.5 L)
5 limes
2½ tablespoons sugar
1 small handful fresh mint

PREPARATION

1. Halve the limes and squeeze out the juice.

2. Stir the sugar with the lime juice until it has dissolved.

3. Wash the mint, shake it dry, and finely chop the mint leaves. Stir this with the lime juice. Dilute with 6½ cups of water and serve on ice.

 **SCOTT'S TIP:**
For our fresh water, or *agua frescas*, I have a general tip: You can also use this drink as a concentrate. Dilute with less water and serve as a "spritz" with mineral or soda water.

Lime-Mint Drink (r.), Hibiscus Petal Drink (recipe page 37) and Watermelon Drink (recipe page 36)

AGUA FRESCA DE SANDÍA
WATERMELON DRINK

This juice can be prepared in large quantities. When chilled well, this drink can last for up to one week. You will get the best results with a food processor or with a hand blender.

PRODUCES ABOUT 1½ QUARTS (1½ L)
2¼ pounds (1 kg) watermelon
1½ tablespoons sugar

PREPARATION

1. Remove the melon from the husk and get rid of the seeds, then dice.

2. Puree the diced melon with the sugar and 2 cups (500 ml) water in the food processor or in the blender.

3. Press the puree through a very fine strainer and squeeze the pulp as well as you can through the strainer.

4. Stir in another 2 cups (500 ml) water and chill until served.

AGUA FRESCA DE JAMAICA
HIBISCUS PETAL DRINK

Finely aromatic, extremely refreshing, and has a great color—it is no wonder that the Mexicans love this drink. They can prepare this drink in large quantities because it can be refrigerated for up to two weeks.

PRODUCES ABOUT 1 QUART (1 L)

¾ teaspoon (4 g) hibiscus petal blossoms (found in Asian markets)

2½ tablespoons sugar

WHEN SERVING:
limes

PREPARATION

1. In a pot, bring the hibiscus petals with the sugar and 3½ cups (350 ml) water to a boil. Poach for one minute, remove from the stove, and then let them infuse for at least one hour.

2. Strain with a very fine sieve or strainer in a bowl. Carefully crush the blossoms. Dilute with 2¾ cups (650 ml) cold water and chill until served.

3. This drink can also be served on ice, garnished with slices of limes.

AGUA FRESCA DE MELÓN
MELON DRINK

When they are ripe, cantaloupe melons sink in a little at the stalk handle and then faintly smell like fresh fruit. Incidentally, they also have an essentially high amount of beta-carotene, like oranges, contain a lot of vitamins A and C, and because of this, they are not only delicious, but also very healthy.

PRODUCES ABOUT 1 QUART (1 L)

2¼ pounds (1 kg) cantaloupe melon
1½ tablespoons sugar

PREPARATION

1. Remove the skin and seeds from the melon. Cut the pulp into cubes.

2. Puree the melon cubes with sugar and 2 cups (500 ml) water in a food processor or blender.

3. Press the puree through a very fine sieve or strainer and squeeze the pulp as well as you can.

4. Stir in another 2 cups (500 ml) water. Chill until served.

 SCOTT'S TIP:

The perfect gateway drug for Agua frescas are, in my opinion, melons. Because they belong in America and also in Europe in every breakfast buffet. One can make delicious, refreshing, and healthy juice from these melons, which is a small surprise for the host.

Rice Milk Frappé (vo., recipe page 41),
Tamarind Drink (hi. li. recipe page 40), and Melon Drink (hi. re.)

AGUA FRESCA DE TAMARINDO
TAMARIND DRINK

Tamarind is not only found in Asia, but in Mexico as well, and is very popular. If you have not yet had the courage to try this unusual, sour-herbed flavor, try using it with this Agua frescas classic. You can also prepare this drink in large quantities, since it can be refrigerated for up to two weeks.

PRODUCES ABOUT 1 QUART (1 L)
1/3 cup (80 g) tamarind pulp
1/2 cup (100 g) sugar

SERVE WITH:
lemons

PREPARATION

1. Mix together the tamarind pulp and sugar well.

2. Fill with 1 quart (1 L) water and puree in a blender or food processor.

3. Chill and serve with ice cubes and lemon slices.

HORCHATA
RICE MILK FRAPPÉ

For this recipe, you have to allow for a rest time of ideally one day, and it is indeed pretty lavish for a cold drink. This drink can be refrigerated for up to one week and simply tastes heavenly. Before serving, make sure you mix the drink well one last time.

PRODUCES ABOUT 1¼ QUARTS (1¼ L)
2/3 cup (150 g) long grain rice
1/3 cup (80 g) almonds
1 lime
1 cinnamon stick
5 all-spice grains
5 drops of almond extract
vanilla extract
1/3 cup (70 g) sugar, as desired

PREPARATION

1. Finely mince the rice in a food processor or in a blender. Blanch the almonds, peel back the skin, and let them dry for a little while. Wash the lime, dry it, and cut the skin into thin strips. Then place the rice with the almonds, the cinnamon stick, the all-spice grains, and the lime zest into a bowl and coat with 2 cups (500 ml) hot (not boiling) water. Let them infuse with the water for at least eight hours, ideally for an entire night.

2. Remove the cinnamon stick, the allspice grains, and the lime zest.

3. Puree the soaked ingredients in a food processor for five minutes until a fine lump mass has formed.

4. Lay out a very fine sieve or strainer with a fresh kitchen towel and hang it over a bowl. Pour in the rice mass and press it through the sieve or strainer with a wooden spoon. Finally, lump the cloth together, twist, and squeeze the rest of the mass into the bowl until about 2 cups (500 ml) fluid is produced. Do not use the rest.

5. Dilute with water as desired and sweeten with sugar to flavor. Serve over ice.

SCOTT'S PREMIUM MARGARITA

A good margarita is easy to mix: you merely have to precisely control the measurements and should only buy the best quality ingredients.

PRODUCES ONE COCKTAIL

½ of a natural lime
⅓ oz (4 cl) Reposado tequila
(i.e. Don Julio or Herradura)
⅔ oz (2 cl) cointreau
⅔ oz (2 cl) Rose's Lime Juice

PREPARATION

1. Squeeze out the lime and mix with the other ingredients.

2. In a large cocktail glass, serve over ice with a piece of garnished lime zest.

MARGARITA CLASSIC
THE CLASSIC MARGARITA

A classic found all over the world. In Milagros, this drink is served, like all other drinks, with tequila, without the famous salt ring. I find that salt overpowers the flavor of the tequila. Just try it out!

PRODUCES ONE COCKTAIL

1^1/$_3$ oz (4 cl) tequila
^{2}/$_3$ oz (2 cl) triple sec
^{2}/$_3$ oz (2 cl) Rose's Lime Juice
^{2}/$_3$ oz (2 cl) lime juice

PREPARATION

1. Mix all of the ingredients in a chilled shaker.

2. Serve in a chilled cocktail glass over ice. Alternatively can be served with crushed ice (see the Mango Margarita).

MARGARITA DE MANGO
MANGO MARGARITA

For this recipe, we use mango puree in the restaurant, which unfortunately, does not exist in frozen form in Germany. You can, of course, use fresh mangos, which can be quickly finely pureed in a blender.

PRODUCES ONE COCKTAIL

4¾ oz (14 cl) 100% Agave tequila
⅔ oz (2 cl) triple sec
⅔ oz (2 cl) Rose's Lime Juice
⅔ oz (2 cl) lime juice
⅔ oz (2 cl) mango puree (canned)

PREPARATION

1. Mix together all of the ingredients.

2. Serve in a large cocktail glass over ice. Alternatively, blend all of the ingredients together with eight ice cubes in a blender until the ice is crushed.

AZTECA
MANGO-LIME COCKTAIL WITH TEQUILA

Our version of Azteca is not made with Kahlúa liquor,
but rather tastes fruity-fresh.

PRODUCES ONE COCKTAIL

½ lime
1 ripe mango
²/₃ oz (2 cl) lime juice
4¾ oz (14 cl) 100% Agave tequila
²/₃ oz (2 cl) mango puree (canned)

PREPARATION

1. Chill a whiskey glass.

2. Peel the lime and mince very finely. Peel the mango and finely dice.

3. Fill the whiskey glass with crushed ice and stir in the rest of the ingredients.

LONG LIVE THE MEXICAN SALSA!

Dips and Chips

GUACAMOLE
AVOCADO DIP

This dip surely belongs to one of the most famous dishes from Mexico and cannot, of course, be allowed to be missing from this cookbook. Guacamole is a good first step toward light, spicy Mexican cuisine.

PRODUCES ABOUT 1 CUP
(250 g)
1 shallot
½ Serrano chili pepper
1 small garlic clove
1 bunch cilantro
1 ripe, aromatic avocado (i.e. Hass avocado)
1 lime
salt

PREPARATION

1. Peel the shallot and finely mince. Wearing kitchen gloves, finely chop the Serrano chili pepper. It should not be too spicy, so cut the chili lengthwise and remove the seeds. Peel the garlic clove and finely chop it. Wash the cilantro, shake it dry, and finely chop the leaves. Shell the avocado and mash the pulp.

2. Divide the lime into thirds and squeeze out the juice with your hand, or halve and use a special lime press to squeeze out the juice.

3. Stir all the ingredients together in a bowl and salt. Place the avocado pit in the mix. Cover the bowl with kitchen wrap and store in the refrigerator. Guacamole certainly tastes best when freshly prepared.

 SCOTT'S TIP:
On page 27, we show you how you can prevent your guacamole from discoloring.

Guacamole (r.), Mexican Salsa (recipe page 53),
Mango Salsa recipe page 52), and Tortillas (recipe page 28)

MANGO SALSA (*Salsa with Fresh Mango and Chili*)

This salsa tastes best when prepared with ripe mangos. The color is not an indication of its ripeness, but rather the kind of mango species. Choose mangos that sink in gently after a light squeeze. Some black spots on the skin are a further indication of ripeness. Mangos that have not yet been cut can be taken home and left in a paper bag to ripen.

MAKES ABOUT 1 CUP (250 g)

2 ripe, aromatic mangos
3 scallions or green onions
1 Jalapeño chili pepper
1 tablespoon smoke-dried red pepper (from a glass jar)
½ bunch cilantro
1 lime
2 teaspoons extra virgin olive oil
salt and freshly ground black pepper

PREPARATION

1. Peel the mangos over a large bowl and save the juice. Finely dice the pulp.

2. Clean the scallions, cut just past the light-green part, wash them, and cut them into roulettes.

3. Wearing kitchen gloves, cut the Jalapeño chili pepper in half, lengthwise. According to your desired level of spiciness, remove all or only a few seeds. Finely chop the husk.

4. Lift the smoke-dried red pepper from liquid and dice.

5. Wash the cilantro, shake it dry, and chop the leaves.

6. Wash the lime, dry it, and finely grate the skin, enough for 1 teaspoon. Cut the lime lengthwise into thirds, squeeze with your hand, or cut it into halves and squeeze out juice with a special lime press.

7. Mix all of the ingredients together in a bowl and season with salt and pepper as desired.

MEXICAN SALSA (*Salsa with Tomatoes and Chilies*)

This spicy salsa tastes best when freshly prepared, is a perfect dip with *totopos*, and is a terrific side dish.

MAKES ABOUT 3⅓ CUPS (800 ml)

1¾ pounds (800 g) ripe tomatoes
1 shallot
1 Serrano chili pepper
1 bunch cilantro
1–2 limes, as desired
salt

PREPARATION

1. Remove the stalks from the tomatoes. Wash and halve them. Scrape out the seeds, dice the flesh, and leave them in a colander to drain for twenty minutes.

2. Peel the shallot and chop.

3. Wearing kitchen gloves, cut the Serrano chili pepper in half lengthwise, scrape out the seeds, and finely cut the flesh.

4. Wash the cilantro, shake it dry, and finely chop the leaves.

5. Cut the lime lengthwise into thirds, squeeze with your hand, or cut it into halves and squeeze out juice with a special lime press.

6. Mix all of the ingredients together in a bowl and flavor with salt and lemon juice as desired. Serve at room temperature immediately.

GREEN SALSA (*Tomatillo-Cilantro Salsa*)

Because this salsa freezes perfectly, you can prepare it in huge quantities.

PRODUCES ABOUT 3 CUPS (700 ml)

1½ pounds (650 g) tomatillos (green tomatoes, canned)
1 Serrano chili pepper
1 medium-sized garlic clove
1 bunch cilantro
1 small onion
salt

PREPARATION

1. Drain the tomatillos and save the liquid. Chop the tomatillos.

2. Wearing kitchen gloves, halve the Serrano chili pepper lengthwise, remove the seeds, and chop coarsely.

3. Peel the garlic clove and chop coarsely.

4. Wash the cilantro, shake it dry, and chop the leaves coarsely.

5. Peel the onion and chop coarsely as well.

6. Blend two tablespoons of the tomatillo liquid, chilies, garlic, and onions with a hand blender or with a regular blender. Then stir in the tomatillos and process everything into a smooth puree. Season with salt and serve or freeze.

 SCOTT'S TIP:

Tomatillos are not, say, special tomatoes, but rather, they are relatives of the Cape gooseberry, also known as the *Physalis peruviana*. Its tangy-sour flavor is typical for real Mexican cuisine. They grow very well in gardens.

`CHILI SALSA

With these ingredients, you might wonder why a list of spices like allspice, clove, and cinnamon, reminds you more of Christmas than a spicy salsa. These are all flavors and aromas that are typically Mexican.

PRODUCES ABOUT 3 CUPS (750 g)

7 Ancho chili peppers
7 Pasilla chili peppers
10 cloves
10 allspice kernels
1 cinnamon stick
1 tablespoon peppercorns
1½ tablespoons salt
1 teaspoon cumin seeds
1 pickled Chipotle chili pepper (Chipotle en adobo)
1 onion
1 garlic clove
1 tablespoon brown sugar
2 cups (500 ml) apple vinegar

PREPARATION

1. Toast the Ancho and Pasilla chili peppers in a pan on medium heat until they develop an aroma, have turned a dark color, and are a bit crispy. Place in a large, heat-resistant bowl and coat with boiling water. Steep until the water cools down to a lukewarm temperature.

2. Measure out 1 cup (250 ml) of the blanched water and pour into another bowl. Place a sieve over this bowl and squeeze the soaked chili peppers through the sieve. For best results, use a wooden spoon to squeeze out as much pulp as possible from the chili peppers.

3. Grind the cloves, allspice kernels, cinnamon stick, pepper, salt, and cumin with a mortar and pestle or with a spice grinder.

4. Drain the Chipotle en adobo. Peel the onion and chop coarsely. Peel the garlic and finely chop it. Puree the finely ground spices, the garlic, the onion, and the Chipotle chili with a hand blender until smooth.

5. Stir in the apple vinegar. Squeeze the chili puree once again through the sieve or through a food mill and mix with the seasoned chili peppers. Until use, fill the salsa in a jar or freeze it.

SCOTT'S TIP:
Mexicans are chili fans and are familiar with many types, which all taste very different from one another. For this recipe, which is very popular in our restaurant, you can find these different types of chilies online. You can find more of our recommendations in the index.

RED SALSA (*Tomato-Chili Salsa*)

A finely spiced dip, an aromatic salsa, and a zesty side dish for tamales.

PRODUCES ABOUT 2 CUPS
(500 g)
1 pound ripe tomatoes
1 shallot
1 small garlic clove
1 tablespoon instant granular broth
1 Serrano chili pepper
1–2 tablespoons vegetable oil
salt and freshly ground black pepper

PREPARATION

1. Remove the stalks of the tomatoes. Wash the tomatoes and chop coarsely.

2. Peel the shallot and garlic clove and chop coarsely as well.

3. Stir in ¼ cup of hot water with the instant broth.

4. Wearing kitchen gloves, halve the Serrano chili peppers lengthwise, remove the seeds, and chop the peppers coarsely.

5. Finely mash the tomatoes, shallots, garlic, and chili pieces together with the broth with the help of a hand blender.

6. Warm up the vegetable oil in a small pot until it is hot, but make sure it is not frying. Stir in the tomato puree and let it simmer on medium heat for twenty minutes until the mass turns darker and condenses. Boldly season the mix one last time.

Tomato-Chili Salsa (r.), Tomato-Cilantro Salsa (recipe page 54), Chili Salsa (recipe page 55), and Tortillas (recipe page 28)

PUMPKIN SEED PUREE DIP

Pumpkin seeds are a good source of vitamins and minerals, and they provide a lot of protein. Thus this dip is not only delicious, but also really healthy in moderation.

PRODUCES ABOUT 1¼ CUPS (300 g)
1 medium-sized tomato
1 small garlic clove
1 cup (250 g) shucked pumpkin seeds
½ Habanero chili pepper
½ teaspoon instant granular broth
1 tablespoon orange juice
1 tablespoon grapefruit juice
1 squirt lime juice, as desired
1 pinch of cinnamon
1 small shallot
½ bunch chives
1 bunch cilantro
salt
tortillas or Totopos (page 28) when serving

PREPARATION

1. Wash the tomato and halve. Brown the unpeeled garlic clove together with the flat surface facing downward in a pan on medium heat for a few minutes. Watch the pan so that the garlic does not burn, otherwise, it will become bitter. Take the clove out of the pan, peel the garlic, and puree both with a hand blender or food processor until smooth.

2. Toast the pumpkin seeds and Habanero chili pepper in a cast-iron skillet on high-heat for a few minutes and make sure to stir well. Sift the pumpkin seeds and shake well so that the leftover shell residue is removed. Let the pumpkin seeds cool. Then, in a food processor or with a mortar and pestle, grind the seeds and stir in the salt and the cinnamon. This should form a coarsely granulated mass, which sticks together well when dipping. Wearing kitchen gloves, halve the chili pepper lengthwise, remove the seeds, finely chop the chili pepper, and put it aside.

3. With three tablespoons hot water stir the instant broth with the orange and grapefruit juice, add in the chili pepper, and puree everything. As desired, flavor with a squirt of lime juice. Now, stir this liquid mass in the puree into two portions.

4. Peel the shallot and finely chop it. Wash the herbs and shake them dry. Cut the chives into fine roulettes and finely chop the leaves of the cilantro. Stir everything into the dip, salt as needed, and pour into a small bowl.

SCOTT'S TIP:
This dip can be prepared in advance up until step three. The puree lasts in an air-tight container in the refrigerator for about three days. Before the food arrangement, simply bring it to room temperature and then continue from step four.

SALSA DE CHILE HABANERO
HABANERO CHILI SALSA

Here is an original recipe from our restaurant, which we of course prepare in large quantities because our guests really love this rather spicy sauce. You can easily freeze it for many months, preferably in two containers, since this amount is enough for eight people. The consistency is best if you let it defrost overnight in the refrigerator before serving. We reveal to you where we shop in the index.

PRODUCES ABOUT 2 CUPS (500 ml)

5 orange-colored Habanero chili peppers
1 garlic clove
1 shallot
1 orange
1 grapefruit
several drops of lime juice, as desired
¾ cup orange-colored Habanero pulp
salt

PREPARATION

1. Brown all of the Habanero chili peppers in a cast-iron skillet on medium heat. Let them cool down.

2. Meanwhile, peel the garlic clove and the shallot and finely chop them.

3. Squeeze out all of the juice from the citrus fruits.

4. Now, puree all of the ingredients with a hand blender, with a mortar, or in a food processor. Salt as desired.

 SCOTT'S TIP:

The jazzy color of Habaneros is simply appetizing. If we freeze the dip, we still add some fresh chilies to it before serving. With this small trick, we bring the color back into the dip, which is somewhat lost when freezing.

SALSA DE CHIPOTLE
CHIPOTLE SALSA

The Chipotle en adobo is a Jalapeño chili pepper that is smoked. Through this process, it has a very distinct, almost bacon-link aroma. It is also called a "butcher's batch."

PRODUCES ABOUT 2½ CUPS (600 ml)

3 tomatoes
1 onion
1–2 garlic cloves
3 pickled Chipotle chili peppers (Chipotle en adobo)
1–2 tablespoons honey
½ cup (100 ml) red wine

PREPARATION

1. Brown the tomatoes and the whole, unpeeled onion on all sides in a pan on medium heat for fifteen minutes until they are brown and the tomato skin bubbles off.

2. Peel the onion and the garlic cloves. Coarsely chop these together with the tomatoes.

3. Mash with the rest of the ingredients in a normal blender or with a hand blender until the salsa has a smooth consistency.

CILANTRO-LIME VINAIGRETTE

This dressing lasts up to two weeks in the refrigerator. Revive it with some cilantro leaves before you serve it.

PRODUCES ABOUT 3⅓ CUPS (800 ml)

2 bunches cilantro
2 limes (1 of them should be natural)
⅓ cup (60 ml) apple vinegar
⅓ cup (60 ml) olive oil
½ tablespoon tarragon mustard
salt and freshly ground black pepper

PREPARATION

1. Wash the cilantro, shake it dry, and finely chop the leaves.

2. Grate the peel from one lime and set aside. Divide both of the limes lengthwise into thirds and squeeze with your hand; alternatively, halve and squeeze with a special lime press.

3. Froth the apple vinegar with the olive oil and the tarragon mustard with a hand blender until creamy. Stir in the lime juice, salt, and pepper.

4. Stir in the rest of the ingredients with a spoon. Chill until served.

Cilantro-Lime Vinaigrette (r.), Salsa with Habanero Chilies (recipe page 60), and Chipotle Salsa (recipe page 61)

SALSA DE FRIJOL NEGRO Y TOMATE
TOMATO-BEAN SALSA

Something healthy to dip Totopos in, or a hearty side dish for grilled dishes–this salsa is diversely versatile.

PRODUCES ABOUT 2¼ POUNDS (1 kg)

1 pound (500 g) ripe tomatoes
14 oz or ¾ pound (400 g) black beans (canned)
1 red onion
1–2 bunches cilantro
½ bunch smooth parsley
1 small garlic clove
1 large Jalapeño chili pepper
3 limes
1 tablespoon extra virgin olive oil
salt and freshly ground black pepper

PREPARATION

1. Remove the stalks from the tomatoes. Wash the tomatoes and finely chop them. Shower the beans in a strainer with cool water, let them drain, and mince them (do not puree). Peel the onion and finely chop it. Transfer everything into a bowl.

2. Wash the herbs, shake them dry, and finely chop them. Wearing kitchen gloves, halve the Jalapeño chili peppers lengthwise, remove the seeds, and finely chop them. Divide the limes lengthwise into thirds and squeeze with your hand; alternatively, halve and squeeze with a special lime press.

3. Stir everything in with the tomato mix, pour in the olive oil, and spice with salt and pepper.

GETTING STARTED

Snacks and Appetizers

QUESADILLAS
CHEESE TORTILLAS

You can be creative with this recipe. The essentials are corn or wheat-flour tortillas with cheese. As desired, pickled Poblano chili peppers, quickly poached oyster mushrooms, or chicken meat are spread on the tortillas. Fold over the tortillas well, and be sure to be sparing with the filling.

PRODUCES 4 SERVINGS

4 large wheat or cornmeal tortillas
¼ pound (100 g) middle-aged Gouda
⅛ pound (50 g) Feta cheese
⅔ pound (300 g) Carnitas (page 129)
2 tablespoons vegetable oil

WHEN SERVING:

guacamole (page 51)
Chipotle salsa (page 61)
or crème fraîche

PREPARATION

1. Preheat the oven to 350°F (180°C). Lay out the tortillas on a work surface.

2. Grate or crumble the cheese and sprinkle over the tortillas.

3. Spread the Carnitas on the tortillas. Fold over the tortillas. Grease a grill pan with some oil and bake the quesadillas on each side until golden brown. Then divide into thirds and arrange on large plates.

4. Serve with guacamole or Chipotle salsa, or simply serve with crème fraîche for dipping.

FRIJOLES BORRACHOS
BACON BEANS

This hearty bean dish tastes even better after a few days than when fresh.

PRODUCES 4 SERVINGS

½ pound (250 g) dried pinto beans
⅔ cup (150 ml) beer
1 Poblano chili pepper (around ½ cup/120g)
1 ripe, aromatic tomato
2¾ oz (80 g) bacon
2¾ oz (80 g) whole Chorizo sausage
1 shallot
1–2 small garlic cloves
1 Jalapeño chili pepper
1 pinch cumin seeds
1 pinch oregano
salt and freshly ground black pepper

PREPARATION

1. Sort the pinto beans. Put them in a pot, coat them with 1 quart (1 L) water, and let them come to a boil once. Remove from the stove and let it stand for at least two hours while covered. Alternatively, soak in cold water for at least twelve hours. Do not use the beans that are floating on the surface of the water or the water itself.

2. Put on the soaked pinto beans with 2 cups (500 ml) water with the beer in a pot. Bring to a boil once, then poach for about one and a half hours on low heat while covered until the pinto beans turn soft, but have not yet burst. In the meantime, check the liquid contents and pour in more water, as desired.

3. Brown the Poblano chili in a coated pan on medium heat for five minutes. Wash the tomato, halve, and with the cut surface facing upwards, brown for five minutes. Finely dice the bacon and bake in a coated pan on a medium temperature until crispy. Brown the Chorizo in the bacon fat. Leave both to drain on kitchen towel or paper towel.

4. Peel the shallot and the garlic clove(s) and chop. Chop the Jalapeño chili pepper. Wearing kitchen gloves, remove the white membrane from the Poblano chili pepper, remove the seeds, and finely chop the chili pepper. Stew the shallot and chili pepper pieces on medium heat in one and a half tablespoons sausage fat (do not use the rest) for eight minutes until they are glazed, then stir in the garlic pieces.

5. Peel the skin of the tomato, remove the stalks and the seeds, then chop the pulp. Stir in the vegetables and simmer on low heat.

6. Meanwhile, carefully brown the cumin seeds and the oregano in a coated pan, then grind.

7. Divide the Chorizo lengthwise into fourths and dice. Stir the bacon, the beans, and the spices into the sauce. Continue to simmer and stir for about ten minutes until the aromas combine. At the end, spice with salt and pepper.

FRIJOLES VEGETARIANOS
BEANS WITH VEGETABLES
Frijoles, or beans, are enjoyable without meat as well.

PRODUCES 4 SERVINGS

1¾ oz (50 g) dried Italian kidney beans
1 onion
2 garlic cloves
1 pinch cumin seeds
1 pinch of oregano
1 bell pepper of your choice
1 large plum tomato
1 Jalapeño chili pepper
1½ tablespoons olive oil
½ cube vegetable bouillon
½ teaspoons pickled Chipotle chili pepper (Chipotle en adobo)
2 medium-sized potatoes
1 zucchini
1 carrot
1 plantain
salt and freshly ground black pepper

PREPARATION

1. Sort the kidney beans. Put them in a pot, coat them with 1 quart (1 L) water, and let them come to a boil once. Remove from the stove and let it stand covered for at least two hours. Alternatively, soak in cold water for at least twelve hours. Do not use the beans that are floating on the surface of the water or the water itself.

2. Peel the onion and the garlic cloves. Coarsely chop the onion and the garlic cloves. Put half of the chopped onion with the chopped garlic cloves and the soaked beans in a pot, coat them with water, let them come to a boil once, then let it simmer for about one hour on low heat while stirring often until the beans are soft, but have not burst. Refill with hot water as needed. Drain the beans, save two-thirds of a cup of the poached water, and let the beans dry.

3. Brown the cumin seeds and the oregano in a cast-iron skillet on low heat and grind out some pepper onto the pan.

4. Wash the bell pepper, halve, clean, and dice. Remove the stalks of the tomato. Wash the tomato, halve, remove the seeds, and dice. Wearing kitchen gloves, halve the Jalapeño chili pepper lengthwise, remove the seeds, and finely chop the pulp.

5. Heat the olive oil in a pan. Crush the rest of the garlic clove. Cook the vegetables with the rest of the onion pieces and the spices on low heat until the onions are glazed. Then stir in the poached beans.

6. Finely puree the poached bean liquid with the Chipotle en adobo. Peel the potatoes and finely dice. Wash the zucchini, clean, and dice. Peel the carrots and finely dice. Peel the plantain and finely dice.

7. Stir in the vegetables with the poached bean liquid with the beans and let them simmer for another twenty minutes until the potatoes are soft. Salt and serve.

FLAUTAS DE QUESO
TAQUITOS WITH A CHEESE FILLING

Mexicans are very creative when it comes to tortillas. They are rolled, coated, or, like in this recipe, deep-fried.

PRODUCES 4 SERVINGS

12 small cornmeal tortillas
1 cup (200 ml) vegetable oil for deep-frying
2/3 pound (300 g) boiled chicken meat
¼ pound (100 g) Gouda cheese
1/8 pound (50 g) Feta cheese
salt and freshly ground black pepper
toothpicks

PREPARATION

1. In a cast-iron skillet, gently roast the tortillas in vegetable oil on both sides very quickly. Let them dry on a kitchen towel or paper towel. They should still be relatively soft, so that they can still roll well.

2. Pick apart the chicken meat into pieces, crumble the cheese or finely grate, and mix the two together. Salt and pepper as desired.

3. Spread the filling on the tortillas, roll, and pin up the borders with toothpicks, so that the filling cannot fall out.

4. Heat the vegetable oil once more in the pan. Deep fry the rolled tortillas quickly while constantly turning until they are golden-brown and crispy.

MOLLETES CON CHORIZO Y FRIJOLES NEGROS REFRITOS
BREAD WITH CHORIZO AND BEANS

Here, we will use a classic from Mexican cuisine: black bean puree.

PRODUCES 4 SERVINGS

½ pound (250 g) black beans
2½ cups (600 ml) chicken broth
1 Jalapeño chili pepper
1 onion
¼ cup lard
1 fresh baguette
14 oz (400 g) Chorizo sausage
salt and freshly ground black pepper

PREPARATION

1. Sort the black beans and soak in water overnight. Drain and sort out the beans once more. Then cover them with the chicken broth in a pot. Put the whole Jalapeño chili pepper in boiling water. Peel the onion, finely chop it, and stir it in the pot as well. Let the beans come to a boil once, then softly poach on low heat for about one hour while covered. Meanwhile, check the liquid contents and pour in more hot water as needed.

2. Puree the poached beans with a hand blender or in a food processor. Melt the lard in a large pan. Fold the bean puree into the lard and scramble well. Spice as desired.

3. Preheat the oven to 250°F (120°C). Cut the baguette diagonally into twelve slices. Brown lightly in the oven. Do not turn off the oven. Spread the baguette slices with the bean puree.

4. Cut the Chorizo into slices and spread onto the baguette. Heat the baguette slices for another few minutes in the oven until the Chorizo sausage is warm. Serve immediately.

ESQUITES
CORN SALAD

If you want to use fresh corn for this corn salad, look for ears of corn with intact grains. Wash the ears thoroughly. Then scrape the grains directly into a large bowl with the back of a knife. Blanch the kernels and then use. This goes wonderfully with grilled dishes.

PRODUCES 4 SERVINGS

½ pickled Poblano chili pepper (canned)
14 oz (400 g) canned corn (5 ears of corn)
½ cup (120 ml) olive oil
1 red bell pepper
1 bunch scallions
3 limes
2 ripe, aromatic avocados
salt and freshly ground black pepper

WHILE SERVING

Parmesan, sour cream, cayenne pepper, tortilla chips

PREPARATION

1. Brown the Poblano chili peppers in a cast-iron skillet on medium heat for five minutes.

2. Drain the canned corn or the blanched corn. Warm up the olive oil in a pan on medium heat. Brown the corn with salt and pepper for five minutes while stirring often, so that it does not burn. Transfer into a large bowl.

3. Wash the bell pepper, halve, clean, finely dice, and put with the corn grains. Clean the scallions, wash them, cut them diagonally into roulettes, and stir these in as well. Wearing kitchen gloves, remove the white membrane from the roasted Poblano chili pepper, halve, remove the seeds, and finely dice. Put with the corn grains. Spice up the vegetables as desired and let them infuse with flavor.

4. In the meantime, squeeze the limes. Shell the avocados, remove the pits, and finely dice. Combine with the lime juice and then fold into the corn.

5. Serve the corn salad with Parmesan, sour cream, cayenne pepper, and tortilla chips as desired.

 **SCOTT'S TIP:**
If you still have leftovers of Salpicón (page 108), then you can also use it as a side dish for this recipe.

SOPA DE TORTILLA
VEGETABLE SOUP WITH TORTILLA CHIPS

This soup almost tastes better as warmed-up leftovers than when freshly prepared. In Mexico, many households do not have electric stoves, so they fry food over open gas flames. This frying process intensifies the aroma of garlic, onions, chilies, tomatoes, and gives them a finely spiced, smoky aroma.

PRODUCES 4 SERVINGS

2 small Pasilla chili peppers
1 small garlic clove
1 small onion
1 pound (500 g) ripe tomatoes
1 tablespoon vegetable oil
1½ quarts (1½ L) chicken broth
1²/₃ cups (400 g) Verdura asadas (page 93)
salt and freshly ground black pepper

WHILE SERVING:

1 ripe, aromatic avocado (i.e., a Hass avocado)
limes
tortilla chips

SCOTT'S TIP:

You can prepare this soup well up until step six, and until use, simply place in a cool setting. Overall, the soup lasts for up to three days in the refrigerator.

PREPARATION

1. Fry the chili peppers on both sides on low heat in a cast-iron skillet until they darken somewhat. Peel the garlic clove and the onion. Coarsely chop the onion, add both of them together, and let them brown a bit. Then place these aside.

2. Wash the tomatoes, remove the stalks, and halve. With the cut side facing downward, fry for about five minutes until they darken, but are not yet soft.

3. Coat one of the Pasilla chili peppers with hot water and leave them covered for thirty minutes, then drain the water. Let the chili peppers dry.

4. Process the roasted, soaked Pasilla chili peppers with the garlic, onion pieces, and tomato halves in a blender or with a hand blender until smoothly pureed, and then salt.

5. Heat the oil in a pan. Simmer the chili-tomato puree on medium heat for five minutes until it darkens and the flavor intensifies.

6. Heat the chicken broth in a pot. Stir in the puree and let it come to a boil once. Now, add the grilled vegetables and simmer for five minutes while covered, so that the aromas blend with each other.

7. Shell the avocado, remove the pit, and cut the pulp into fine strips. Wash the limes with cold water and divide into eighths. Cut the extra Pasilla chili pepper into fine rings. Salt and pepper the soup and serve it on the side with tortilla chips, avocado strips, the lime chunks, and chili rings.

POZOLE ROJO
MEXICAN CORN STEW

Hominy are dried and shucked corn grains. They were one of the first foods that the European settlers had the courage to try from the new American continent.

PRODUCES 4 SERVINGS

1 pound (500 g) pork shoulder, ideally with the bone
1 tablespoon vegetable oil
1 small carrot
1 onion
2 pale celery stalks
1 bouquet garni (see Scott's Tip)
1 Ancho chili pepper
½ Pasilla chili pepper
2 plum tomatoes
1 small garlic clove
½ pound (250 g) hominy
salt

WHILE SERVING:
Salpicón (page 108)
limes
Totopos (page 28)

SCOTT'S TIP:
Our bouquet garni consists of two parsley stalks, two bay leaves, four skinned garlic cloves, two thyme sprigs, and six peppercorns wrapped in a small cooking bag.

PREPARATION

1. Rinse off the meat, dab it dry with a paper towel, and roast gently in hot oil on all sides. Pour in 1 quart (1 L) hot water.

2. Peel the carrot and chop. Peel the onion, put aside one half, and chop the other half. Wash the pale celery stalks, shake them dry, de-stalk, and chop. Put the bouquet garni with the rest of the vegetables in the broth and let it well up. Salt the broth, and let it simmer on the lowest heat for two hours while covered. Skim off the foam if desired.

3. Pour the soup through a sieve. Pluck the meat into pieces, fill a small bowl, and let it cool through overnight in the refrigerator. If a fat layer forms on top of the soup, pick this off and do not use.

4. Brown both types of chili peppers in a cast-iron skillet on a medium temperature for five minutes. Then, wearing kitchen gloves, halve lengthwise and remove the seeds. Put the chili peppers in a heat-resistant bowl, blanch with boiling water, and steep for thirty minutes.

5. Meanwhile, remove the stalks from the tomatoes, wash them, and halve. Peel the garlic cloves. Chop the rest of the onion and brown with the tomato and the garlic in a pan.

6. Dry the soaked chili peppers and with some blanched water, finely mash with a hand blender or with a food processor. Press through a very fine sieve into the broth.

7. Mince the tomatoes, the garlic, and the onion with a hand blender and put together with the broth as well.

8. Now, stir in the hominy. Let the broth well up once and let it simmer for forty-five minutes. Add the meat and let it simmer for another fifteen minutes. Serve the soup with lime chunks, Totopos, and diced cubes of cheese.

SOPA AVOCADO
SOUP WITH GUACAMOLE AND TOMATILLOS
(Mexican Tomatoes)

We could definitely get fresh tomatillos from the Munich daily market, but they are so expensive that, as an exception, we use canned ones in this dish.

PRODUCES ABOUT 1 QUART (1 L)

¼ pound (100 g) tomatillos (canned)
½ Serrano chili pepper
1 thick bunch scallions
½ garlic clove
1 teaspoon vegetable oil
1 quart (1 L) chicken or vegetable broth
2 limes
2 ripe avocados
1 small bunch cilantro
salt

WHEN SERVING:
⅔ cup (150 g) crème fraîche
Totopos (page 28)
Mexican Salsa (page 53)

PREPARATION

1. Let the tomatillos dry and then coarsely chop them. Wearing kitchen gloves, remove the seeds and white membrane from the Serrano chili pepper and coarsely chop it. Clean the scallions, wash them, and coarsely chop them. Peel the garlic clove and coarsely chop it.

2. Heat the oil in a pot and lightly brown the tomatillos with the Serrano chili pepper, the scallions, and the garlic on a low temperature in the oil. Pour in the broth. Let the pot well up once and let it simmer for fifteen to twenty minutes until the vegetables are soft.

3. Puree the soup with a hand blender or in a food processor until soft. Let it cool down, then cool overnight or for at least four hours.

4. Squeeze the limes before serving, shell the avocados, remove the pits, and dice the pulp. Wash the cilantro, shake it dry, and finely chop the leaves.

5. Stir in the lime juice, avocado cubes, and cilantro into the cooled soup and finely puree with a hand blender or in a food processor. Salt as desired.

6. Serve with crème fraîche, Totopos, and Mexican salsa.

SOPA DE CILANTRO
CILANTRO SOUP

There are actually only two opinions when it comes to the topic of cilantro: either you love its light, soapy aroma, or you feel like it is unbearable, even in the smallest dose. Mexicans love it.

PRODUCES ABOUT 1 QUART (1 L)

¼ Serrano chili pepper
1 small zucchini
2 potatoes
1 quart (1 L) chicken broth
1 small leek
½ bunch scallions
1 garlic clove
2 tablespoons butter
3 bunches cilantro
⅓ cup (80 g) crème fraîche
salt and freshly ground black pepper

WHEN SERVING

cilantro
¼ pound Feta cheese
Totopos (page 28)

PREPARATION

1. Brown the Serrano chili pepper in a cast-iron skilled on medium heat for five minutes. Then, wearing kitchen gloves, peel the skin and remove the seeds. Chop the pulp and put aside.

2. Remove the ends of the zucchini, wash it, and dice. Peel the potatoes and dice. Heat both up in a pot with the chicken broth, let it well up once, and then simmer for twenty minutes until the vegetables are soft.

3. Clean the leek, cut it lengthwise, wash it thoroughly, and coarsely chop it. Clean the scallions, wash them, and coarsely chop them. Peel the garlic and coarsely chop it as well.

4. Heat up the butter in a pan. Cook the Serrano chili pepper pieces with the leek, the scallions, and the garlic for a few minutes until they are glazed. Then stir in the soup.

5. Wash the cilantro, shake it dry, and finely puree half of the leaves with ½ cup (100 ml) of the broth. Mix in the soup. Stir in the rest of the cilantro and the crème fraîche. Salt and pepper the soup.

6. Dice the Feta, and if you would like, stick the Feta cubes onto short satay sticks and serve with Totopos and cilantro leaves.

 SCOTT'S TIP:
If you are a cilantro fan, try this soup as a chilled soup in the hot summer if you are not very hungry, but still have somewhat of a hearty appetite. When chilled, this soup lasts for several days.

ON THE GRILL

Grilled Dishes

ARRACHERA GRILLED BEEF

The actual preparation is pretty quick. Make sure to calculate more time because this grilled classic, which can also qualify as a filling, tastes the best when it is marinated overnight.

PRODUCES 4–6 SERVINGS

1 tablespoon cumin seeds
2 Serrano chili peppers
1 small garlic clove
2 limes
1 teaspoon steak spice
¾ cup (180 ml) olive oil
1 bunch cilantro
2¼ pounds entrecôte (steak)

PREPARATION

1. Roast the cumin seeds in a cast-iron skillet on very low heat for five minutes until they release an aroma. Fill them in a food processor, mortar, or blender.

2. Wearing kitchen gloves, halve the Serrano chili peppers lengthwise and remove the seeds, white membrane, and the stem. Put with the cumin seeds.

3. Peel the garlic clove. Squeeze out the limes. Put the garlic clove and the lime juice together with the cumin seeds and puree or grind everything with the steak spice and olive oil.

4. Wash the cilantro, shake it dry, chop the leaves, and stir in the puree. Mix again until a marinade forms.

5. Rinse off the meat and carefully dab it dry with a paper towel. Cut across the grain into ¼–⅓ inch (6–8 millimeter) wide strips. Spread the marinade across the meat strips and roll them up. Then let it infuse with the rest of the marinade in a plastic bag for at least eight hours and up to two days in the refrigerator.

6. Bring the meat to room temperature thirty minutes before grilling and roll the strips apart from one another. Gently brown the meat on the grill on both sides until medium-rare, and, if desired, cut it into fine slices when serving.

PATO ASADO EN ESCABECHE
PICKLED DUCK FILETS

This somewhat sour marinade has a long history and is commonly found in many regions of the world between Italy and the Philippines. Originally, this was only used for fish dishes, but I find that this marinade is exquisite with duck as well.

PRODUCES 4 SERVINGS

4 duck filets without the skin
1 teaspoon salt
2 teaspoons allspice
2 teaspoons oregano
1 onion
2 large carrots
2 tablespoons extra virgin olive oil
2 garlic cloves
¼ cup (60 ml) apple vinegar
1 cup (250 ml) chicken broth
3 pickled Jalapeño chili peppers (canned)
freshly ground black peppers

PREPARATION

1. Rinse off the duck filets and dab them dry. Combine together the salt, oregano, allspice, and pepper in a small bowl. Rub half of the herb mix onto the filets and put aside.

2. Peel the onion and cut it into ⅕ inch (5 mm) thick slices. Peel the carrots and cut it diagonally into ⅕ inch (5 mm) wide slices. Heat up the olive oil in a large pan. Cook the onions and carrots on medium heat while stirring regularly until the onion has browned after about eight minutes.

3. Peel the garlic cloves, halve, stir in the vegetables, and cook them for one minute, then put in the rest of the herb mix. Pour in the apple vinegar and the chicken broth and stir.

4. Wearing kitchen gloves, halve the Jalapeño chili peppers lengthwise, remove the seeds, and cut them into thin rings. Stir into the pan as well.

5. Grill the duck filets on medium heat for about ten minutes until they are cooked all the way through. Serve with the escabeche.

POLLO A LA PARRILLA
GRILLED CHICKEN

The Mexican version of this green sauce, tomatillo-cilantro salsa or *salsa verde*, is suitable by itself and is also perfect with a lot of toasted pumpkin seeds and the unusually aromatic *mole verde*.

PRODUCES 4 SERVINGS

2 chicken breast filets
3 tablespoons extra virgin olive oil
1 tablespoon oregano
salt and freshly ground black pepper

WHEN SERVING:
tomatillo-cilantro salsa or *salsa verde* (page 54)
or *mole verde* (page 96)

PREPARATION

1. Mix the olive oil with the oregano for the chicken breast filets and spice generously. Rub this mix onto the meat.

2. Lightly roast the meat on the grill for ten minutes and flip the meat over halfway through. Check the cooking temperature: the chicken breast has to be fully cooked through.

3. Serve with *salsa verde* or *mole verde*.

SCOTT'S TIP:
This recipe can be made successfully even by grilling rookies and is a terrific first step toward Mexican cuisine. If you still have not dared to venture into the making of a mole because the ingredients seem too exotic, I promise you that you will like this combination.

BARBACOA DE POLLO
CHICKEN IN A CHILI MARINADE

Chili peppers and herbs belong in this barbacoa sauce, which also goes well with beef. This is a really hearty dish.

PRODUCES 4 SERVINGS

1/3 cup (70 g) sugar
1/3 cup (70 g) salt
5 allspice grains
20 peppercorns
1 chicken, kitchen-ready and halved
1 tablespoon vegetable oil
1¼ cups (300 ml) chili salsa (page 55)
1 teaspoon oregano

WHEN SERVING:
chili salsa (page 55) or tomatillo-cilantro salsa (page 54)

PREPARATION

1. Dissolve the sugar and salt in a bowl with 2 quarts (2 L) water. Grind the allspice grains and peppercorns and stir them into the bowl. Lay the chicken into the marinade and chill for at least four hours.

2. Take the chicken out of the marinade, rinse off, and dab it dry with a paper towel. Do not use the rest of the marinade.

3. Let the vegetable oil get very hot in a pan. Pour in the chili salsa; it should really sizzle. Stir in the oregano. Simmer the salsa on very low heat for fifteen minutes until it darkens and thickens. Let it cool down completely.

4. Fill up a plastic bag with the chicken and the salsa, combine them well, and let them chill for twenty-four hours.

5. Lift the meat out of the salsa and grill. Do not use the rest of the salsa. Serve with tomatillo-cilantro salsa or chili salsa.

PAPAS CON RAJAS
SPICY POTATOES

This delicious dish is suitably outstanding as a filling for tacos and is the perfect side dish.

PRODUCES ABOUT 4 SERVINGS

1²/₃ cups (400 g) pickled Poblano chili peppers
1¾ pounds (800 g) medium-sized potatoes, primarily waxy or a low-starch, boiling potato
1 onion
1 garlic clove
2 tablespoons vegetable oil
½ teaspoons oregano
salt and freshly ground black pepper

WHEN GARNISHING:
parmesan cheese
red-hot paprika powder

PREPARATION

1. Brown the Poblano chili peppers in a cast-iron skillet on medium heat for five minutes.

2. Poach the potatoes in lightly salted water for twenty minutes until they almost become soft. Drain and shock with cold water. As soon as they are cooled, peel and then cut them into 1-inch (2 cm) cubes.

3. Wearing kitchen gloves, remove the white membrane from the Poblano chili pepper, cut it up lengthwise, remove the seeds, and cut it into thin, finger-length strips.

4. Peel the onion and cut it into ultra thin rings. Peel the garlic and chop.

5. Heat up the oil in a large cast-iron skillet. Lightly brown the potato cubes with the onion rings in the pan until the potatoes have taken on a color and the onion rings have caramelized. Stir in the garlic and cook it for two minutes. Now, stir in the Poblano chili peppers and let them warm throughout.

6. Sprinkle the oregano on top and spice with salt and pepper. Serve garnished with parmesan, sour cream, and paprika.

 SCOTT'S TIP:
If you really want it to be spicy, heat up the red-hot paprika powder with a puff of cayenne powder.

VERDURAS ASADAS
GRILLED VEGETABLES

Mexicans love meat, but in this sun-kissed country, one knows, of course, how to prepare delicious vegetables.

PRODUCES 4 SERVINGS

1 pinch of oregano
2 zucchinis
1 onion
1 red onion
1 bunch scallions
1 red bell pepper
1–2 Jalapeño chili peppers
1–2 garlic cloves
$1/3$ cup (80 ml) olive oil
salt and freshly ground black pepper

PREPARATION

1. Brown the oregano in a cast-iron skillet and combine with the ground pepper.

2. Wash the zucchinis, clean, and cut them lengthwise into fine, 2¾ inch-long (7 cm) strips. Peel the onion and cut it into ultra-thin rings. Clean the scallions, wash them, and divide them lengthwise into thirds while also using the green part of the scallions. Halve the pieces lengthwise.

3. Wash the bell pepper, halve, clean, and cut it into fine strips. Wearing kitchen gloves, halve the Jalapeño chili peppers lengthwise, remove the seeds, and cut them into fine rings. Peel the garlic cloves and finely chop them.

4. Mix all of the ingredients in a bowl with the olive oil and let them marinate ideally overnight, or for at least four hours.

5. Salt generously, then roast them on the grill until the vegetable pieces show off brown grill stripes and the onion rings are caramelized.

MOLE POBLANO
MEXICAN CHOCOLATE-CHILI SAUCE

This sauce is known world-wide and tastes especially good in grilled dishes.

PRODUCES 4 SERVINGS

10–11 Pasilla chili peppers
10–11 Mulato chili peppers
8 Ancho chili peppers
¾ pound (350 g) roma tomatoes
2 small garlic cloves
1 onion
½ pound (250 g) roasted peanuts
1½ tablespoons sugar
3 tablespoons sour cream
(alternatively, ½ cup or 100 ml of vegetable oil)
1 teaspoon oregano
½ teaspoon allspice
½ ground cloves
½ teaspoon cinnamon
1 good pinch freshly grated nutmeg
$^1/_3$ cup of raisins
3 tablespoons coffee liqueur (i.e., Kahlúa)
3 tablespoons freshly brewed espresso
1 teaspoon pickled Chipotle chili peppers (Chipotle en adobo)
¼ pound bittersweet chocolate

SCOTT'S TIP:
This sauce requires some preparation, therefore it is worth it to make this in large quantities. Freeze in small portions (i.e., in ice cube form) and defrost when desired.

PREPARATION

1. The chilies are prepared one day before the preparation of the sauce. For this, preheat the oven to 350°F (170°C). Halve the chili peppers lengthwise, remove the seeds and stem, and roast in the oven for twenty minutes until they darken and are somewhat crispy. In a heat-resistant bowl, blanch them with boiling water and let them soak overnight.

2. Drain the chili peppers the next day, rinse well, and coat them once more with boiling water in a bowl.

3. Wash the tomatoes and dab them dry with a paper towel. Warm up a greased pan on high heat. Roast the tomatoes with the garlic and the whole onion for several minutes until the vegetables turn a dark color. Peel the garlic cloves and the onion. Chop everything coarsely and put aside.

4. Work the peanuts in a mortar or with a rolling pin in a plastic bag until mashed completely. Stir in the sugar and put aside.

5. Heat up one tablespoon lard or ¼ of a cup of vegetable oil in a greased pan. Brown the spices and the raisins on very low heat while stirring constantly until the raisins have formed a mass. Remove the pan from the stove immediately, otherwise, the raisins will burn.

6. Mix together the vegetables, the peanut mash, and the spices well in a mortar or with a hand blender. Transfer into a large bowl.

7. Combine the coffee liqueur with the espresso and the Chipotle chili until it forms a smooth paste. Chop the chocolate and let it melt with the coffee mixture while frequently stirring in a water bath, then place this mixture in a bowl.

8. Drain the chili peppers, rinse off with cold water one more time, and let them dry well. Then work this into a smooth, creamy mass with a hand blender. Stir in the rest of the ingredients and finely puree serving sizes with a hand blender.

MOLE VERDE DE OAXACA
MOLE VERDE FROM OAXACA

This famous sauce from the southern part of the country is prepared with pumpkin seeds and lettuce. It is very, very tasty, especially with poultry, but also with tortillas, and they are also budget-friendly—Mexico is not a rich country.

PRODUCES ABOUT 2 QUARTS (2 L)

1 small, crunchy lettuce head
½ pound (250 g) arugula
½ pound (250 g) tomatillos (canned)
1 star anise
1 small bunch scallions
1 garlic clove
1 shallot
1 small, stale roll or piece of baguette
1½ quarts (1½ L) chicken broth
1¼ cups (300 g) shelled pumpkin seeds
salt and freshly ground black pepper

PREPARATION

1. Clean the lettuce head, wash it, shake it dry, and coarsely chop it. Take the tomatillos out from the can and mince as desired. Crush the star anise. Clean the scallions, wash them, use only the white parts of the scallions, and coarsely chop these parts. Peel the garlic clove and the shallot and chop. Grate the stale roll or piece of baguette.

2. Brown the pumpkin seeds underneath the grill or in a pan on very low heat. (Be careful, these burn easily and then turn bitter.)

3. Put the chicken broth in a pot. Stir in all the ingredients, spice, let it boil, and then simmer on the lowest heat until the sauce thickens and becomes creamy after about thirty minutes. In the meantime, stir around the broth constantly.

4. Finely puree the sauce or press through a food mill, then spice as desired.

Mole verde (r.), Tequila Sauce (recipe page 98), and Adobado (recipe page 99)

REDUCCIÓN DE TEQUILA
TEQUILA SAUCE

This sauce is simple to conceive and matches ideally with filet mignon. Use light tequila.

PRODUCES 4 SERVINGS

1 quart (1 L) chicken broth
1 cup (250 g) cream
1 cup (250 g) sugar
¾ cup (180 ml) tequila

PREPARATION

1. Mix all of the ingredients together and poach in a pot on very low heat while stirring frequently for about twenty minutes.

 SCOTT'S TIP:
Tequila is the Mexican miracle elixir. In this sauce, the alcohol has evaporated, and only the agave flavor remains within.

ADOBADO
MARINADE FOR GRILLED MEAT

Spiciness and fruitiness are markers of this very typical Mexican marinade. It is childishly simple to make and adds variety to the grill table.

ENOUGH FOR 2¼ POUNDS (1 KG) MEAT

3–4 garlic cloves
2 teaspoons oregano
½ teaspoon thyme
½ teaspoon cumin powder
2 tablespoons red wine vinegar
2–3 pickled Chipotle chili peppers (Chipotle en adobo)
3 oranges
1 lime
salt and freshly ground black pepper

PREPARATION

1. Peel the garlic cloves and finely chop them. In a bowl, combine the garlic with the spices and stir in the red wine vinegar.

2. Wearing kitchen gloves, finely chop the Chipotle chili and stir into the mixture. Squeeze out the citrus fruits and stir in the juice with the rest of the spices into the bowl with a hand blender, then flavor with salt and pepper.

3. Lay the two and one-quarter pounds meat that you will marinate later (i.e., poultry, steaks, cutlets) in another bowl and then spread a consistent amount of marinade over the meat. Chill the meat in the refrigerator for four to six hours while covered. Mix again afterwards if desired.

 SCOTT'S TIP:
Marinades are perfect for comfortable cooks and for beginners. The long marinating time makes the food about to be grilled soft and juicy. If you do not forget the marinade on the grill, your food will not dry out.

FILET MIGNON CON UNA SALSA REDUCCIÓN DE JAMAICA Y CHIPOTLE
FILET MIGNON WITH A CHIPOTLE REDUCTION SAUCE

This is the new Mexican cuisine with entirely classic aromas. You will find hibiscus petals on almost every table, in addition to Chipotle chili peppers, which have an unmistakable smoky aroma.

PRODUCES 4 SERVINGS

2 cups (500 g) dried hibiscus petals
1 quart (1 kg) sugar
1 cinnamon stick
2 tablespoons pickled Chipotle chili peppers (Chipotle en adobo)
4 filet mignons (about 1¾ pounds or 800g)
2–3 tablespoons olive oil
salt

PREPARATION

1. Draw up a pot with the hibiscus petals in 2 quarts (2 L) water and let it come to a boil once. Press the petals through a sieve. Collect the boiled water.

2. Dissolve the sugar, cinnamon stick, the pickled Chipotle chili pepper, and salt in the boiled water and let them simmer on low heat while stirring frequently without a cover for at least one and a half hours until the sauce reduces and is gooey. Remove the cinnamon stick.

3. Rinse off the filets with cold water ten minutes before serving and carefully dab them dry. Lightly rub them with olive oil. For a medium rare, roast the filets on both sides in olive oil for five minutes, then lift them from the pan, cover them with aluminum foil, and leave them to rest for five minutes. Lightly salt, spread sauce over them, and serve immediately.

 SCOTT'S TIP:
Our spicy potatoes, the Papas con rajas (page 92), go especially well with this dish.

MEDALLONES DE CERDO
PORK MEDALLIONS WITH SALSAS

The Milagros of course serves not only classics, but also its own creations. We are especially proud of this recipe.

PRODUCES 4 SERVINGS

1 pork loin (¾–1 pound/400–500g)

2 oranges

1 lime

⅔ cup (150 g) Annatto paste
(also known as Achiote paste)

When serving:

Chipotle salsa (page 61)

Mango salsa (page 52)

WHEN SERVING:

Chipotle Salsa (page 61)

Mango Salsa (page 52)

PREPARATION

1. Rinse off the pork loin, dab it dry, and cut into fingerbreadth pieces of about 50 grams. Squeeze out the citrus fruit and combine with the Annatto paste. Mix the meat in with the marinade and let it cool overnight while covered.

2. Bring the grilling meat to room temperature. Lift the meat from the marinade (do not use the rest of the marinade) and grill as desired.

3. Serve garnished with Chipotle salsa and mango salsa.

🌶 **Scott's Tip:**

This recipe unifies typical Mexican flavors–citrus fruits, tropical fruit, and spice. The right amount can create a perfectly well-rounded flavor experience. If you have a chance to get to Mexico, definitely try out many types of mangos, which are diverse, from flat and yellow to fat and green. They are simply delicious and very healthy.

AL PASTOR
FRUIT-MARINATED PORK

This dish tastes like a filling that you would find in burritos or like a topping for fine tacos. It is also delicious with Chipotle salsa (page 61). And it goes well with ice-cold beer, of course.

PRODUCES 4 SERVINGS

5 Guajillo chili peppers
4½ pounds (2 kg) pork neck
2 oranges
½ lemon
1 shallot
1 garlic clove
1 pinch of oregano
1 pinch of cumin seed powder
1 pinch of dried, crumbled rosemary
2 cloves
2 tablespoons (30 g) Annatto seeds
¼ cup (60 ml) white wine or apple vinegar
1 cinnamon stick
a few drops of Tabasco
salt and freshly ground black pepper

PREPARATION

1. Roast the Guajillo chili peppers for a few minutes in a pan on medium heat. Then place in a heat-resistant bowl and douse them with hot water. Soak until the water cools down to a lukewarm temperature. Wearing kitchen gloves, lift the peppers out from the water, let them dry, halve lengthwise, and remove the seeds. Coarsely chop them.

2. Cut the pork into finger-length and wide strips.

3. Squeeze out the citrus fruits, peel the shallot, and peel the garlic clove. Puree the Guajillo chili pepper with the citrus juices, the shallot, the garlic, and all the other ingredients in a food processor to form a marinade.

4. Flip the meat strips over in the marinade and let them cool overnight in the refrigerator or for at least twelve hours.

5. Lift the meat out from the marinade and grill them.

 SCOTT'S TIP:
Put pineapple slices in the marinade! Not only do they taste fruity-sweet, but they also are a natural meat softener.

TRADITIONS

Classic Dishes

SALPICÓN
VEGETABLE SALAD

This salad is an aromatic side dish and is also an optimally interesting topping—for example, with frijoles, enchiladas, and meat dishes.

PRODUCES 4 SERVINGS

½ pound (250 g) white or Chinese cabbage
5 oz (150 g) radishes
1 onion
2 bunches chives
2 Serrano chili peppers
2 bunches cilantro
3 limes

PREPARATION

1. Clean the cabbage, wash it, then chop it very finely or shred it. Clean the radishes, wash them, and cut them into fine slices. Peel the onion and chop it. Wash the chives, shake them dry, and cut them into roulettes. Wearing kitchen gloves, halve the Serrano chili peppers lengthwise, remove the seeds, and finely chop the pulp.

2. Combine all of the ingredients in a bowl and chill until serving.

3. Wash the cilantro, shake it dry, and finely chop the leaves. Squeeze out the limes, stir the cilantro and salt into the salad, then serve.

CEBOLLAS ENCURTIDAS
MARINATED ONIONS

With this basic recipe, you can start to do a lot of things: it works well with grilled meat and also works as a filling.

PRODUCES 4 SERVINGS

½ of a garlic clove
½ Serrano chili pepper
1–2 cloves
5 peppercorns
½ teaspoon oregano
1 cup (250 ml) bitter orange juice (alternatively, use orange and grapefruit juice, plus some squirts of lime juice)
1 pound (500 g) onions
coarse sea salt

PREPARATION

1. Brown the garlic for a few minutes on very low heat in a cast-iron skillet with the cut surface facing downward until it is soft. Do not let it burn. Then push out the pulp from the husk.

2. Brown the Serrano chili peppers in a cast-iron skillet for a few minutes on low heat. Let them cool a little bit, then, while wearing kitchen gloves, remove the white membrane from the chilies, cut them up lengthwise, and remove the seeds and stems. Coarsely chop the chilies.

3. Lightly heat the cloves and the peppercorns in a pan, then finely grind them in a mortar or mash them with a rolling pin.

4. Stir in the mashed spices with the oregano, the garlic pulp, and the Serrano chili peppers. Then stir in the bitter orange juice and finely puree everything with a hand blender or in a food processor. Season with one teaspoon sea salt.

5. Peel the onions, cut them into fine rings, and part these into segments. Lay the onion slices into a large bowl and sprinkle on the marinade. Let them infuse for one hour at room temperature.

BURRITOS
ROLLED DOUGH FLAT CAKES

Hardly any dish has been associated so much with the Mexican borders like the burrito. Interestingly, burritos have not been typically Mexican for that long. Because wheat first came during the beginning of the seventeenth century by way of the Spanish conquerors in Mexico.

PRODUCES 4 SERVINGS

4 wheat flour tortillas
¼ pound (120 g) mozzarella
½ pound (200 g) cooked rice
½ pound (200 g) Frijoles borracho or vegetarianos (page 70/71), drained
½ pound (200 g) meat filling as desired (see Scott's Tip)

WHEN SERVING:
crème fraîche
cheese
Mexican salsa

PREPARATION

1. Lightly heat up the tortillas on a grill or in an oven grill until they assume some color.

2. Finely cut the cheese.

3. Lay out the tortillas on a countertop. Coat them first with the rice, then with Frijoles borracho o vegetarianos, and lastly with a meat filling, as desired. Sprinkle the cheese over the tortillas.

4. Now, roll up the tortillas to form cylinders, arrange them onto plates, and serve with cheese, Mexican salsa, and crème fraîche

🔥 SCOTT'S TIP:
As a meat filling, Al pastor (page 105), Arrachera (page 85), Cochinita pibil (page 130), or Carnitas de Pato (page 129) all are outstanding with this dish.

BURRITO DE DESAYUNO
BREAKFAST ROLLS

There are two kinds of tortillas: tortillas made from cornmeal and tortillas made from wheat flour. Wheat flour tortillas are used for burritos. Because these tortillas do not have too much of a flavor by themselves, you can be somewhat hearty with the filling.

PRODUCES 4 SERVINGS

8 eggs
1 thick bunch chives
2 tablespoons butter
4 wheat flour tortillas
¼ pound (120 g) aromatic grating cheese (Gouda)
3–4 tablespoons crème fraîche
½ pound (200 g) Carnitas (page 129)
Papas con rajas (page 92)
½ pound (200 g) Cebollas encurtidas (page 109)
salt and freshly ground black peppers

WHEN SERVING:
Salsa, if desired
guacamole (page 51)
totopos (page 28)

PREPARATION

1. Beat the eggs with three tablespoons water. Wash the chives, shake them dry, and cut them into fine roulettes. Beat the roulettes into the egg wash with an egg beater and then salt and pepper everything generously.

2. Heat the butter in a large cast-iron skillet. Work the eggs slowly into the pan by stirring them into scrambled eggs and then take them out of the pan when they are bound together, but have not yet dried out. Afterwards, put the eggs aside.

3. Lightly heat up the tortillas on a grill or in an oven grill until they assume some color. Grate the cheese.

4. Lay out the tortillas on a countertop and coat them first with the scrambled eggs in the middle. Over this, spread on the meat (Carnitas) or the potatoes (Papas con rajas) onto the eggs, and on top of that, dress this with onions, and as the final step, sprinkle cheese on top and spread the crème fraîche.

5. Roll the tortillas tight to form cylinders. As desired, either halve or wrap them in aluminum foil in order to eat the tortillas by hand.

6. Serve with salsa, guacamole, and totopos.

CREPAS DE HONGO
CRÊPES WITH A MUSHROOM FILLING

Aside from tortillas, you can also add filling in these paper-thin egg pancakes, which are also typically Mexican.

PRODUCES 4 SERVINGS

2 tablespoons butter
²/₃ cup (150 g) flour
²/₃ cup (150 ml) milk
2 eggs
1 bunch cilantro
2 tablespoons vegetable oil
1–2 Pasilla or Arból chili peppers
3 tablespoons extra olive oil
1 onion
1 garlic clove
1¹/₃ pounds (600 g) mushrooms
3 tablespoons flour
⁷/₈ cup (200 ml) milk
½ cup (100 g) crème fraîche
½ cup (120 g) shredded Manchego
salt and freshly ground black pepper

PREPARATION

1. For the crêpes, melt the butter in a small pot. Work the salt, ½ cup (125 ml) milk, and the eggs into the flour with the help of a hand mixer until it forms a thin batter.

2. Wash the cilantro, shake it dry, and finely chop the leaves. Stir in two tablespoons it into the crêpe batter. Let the batter sit at room temperature for one hour while covered, then carefully stir in the rest of the milk, as desired.

3. Heat up some of the vegetable oil. Fry up some of the batter to form a thin crêpe. Repeat this process until all of the batter is used up. Pile the crêpes on top of each other on a large plate.

4. For the filling, cut up the chili peppers lengthwise. While wearing kitchen gloves, remove the white membrane and seeds, and finely chop them. Heat one tablespoon the olive oil in a pan and quickly fry the chilies, then lift them out of the pan and let them dry on a paper towel. Crumble them up afterward.

5. Peel the onion and garlic clove and finely chop them. Heat the rest of the olive oil in a pan. Sauté the onions and garlic in the pan until they are glazed.

6. Clean the mushrooms and finely chop them. Fold the mushrooms into the onion mix, salt, pepper, and then simmer for ten minutes while covered.

7. Combine the milk with the flour into the pan and leave it to simmer on low heat for five minutes while constantly stirring, so that small clumps form. Stir in the crème fraîche und the Manchego and simmer until the sauce forms a creamy consistency. Salt and pepper.

8. Cover the crêpes with the mushroom filling, roll them up, and arrange them on plates with the seams facing downward. Pour the hot cheese sauce over the crêpes and serve.

ALBÓNDIGAS CON SALSA VERDE
MEATBALLS WITH SALSA VERDE (*Tomatillo-Cilantro Salsa*)

With these meatballs, which are poached in Mexico, and not roasted, there are so many regional varieties: with zucchini, with and without hard boiled eggs, with tomatoes, carrots, and finely ground, raw rice instead of breadcrumbs . . . Here is a recipe from Milagros. This tastes great with rice.

PRODUCES 4 SERVINGS

3 tablespoons milk
½ cup (125 g) breadcrumbs
1 cup (250 ml) Salsa verde (page 54)
1 cup (250 ml) beef or chicken broth
5 eggs
1 medium-sized onion
2¼ pounds (1 kg) mixed ground meat
1 bunch cilantro
salt and freshly ground black pepper

PREPARATION

1. Put the milk in a small bowl and soak the breadcrumbs in this.

2. Bring the Salsa verde and the broth to a boil in a medium-sized pot, in which the meatballs should be able to fit later. Then leave them to simmer on very low heat for ten minutes. Salt as desired.

3. Boil three eggs for ten minutes and then chill them with water, then peel and finely chop them. Whisk the rest of the eggs. Peel the onions and finely chop them. Combine the ground meat with the soaked breadcrumbs, the whisked eggs, and the onion pieces in a bowl.

4. Wash the cilantro and shake it dry. Put aside some leaves for decoration, finely chop the rest of the cilantro, and then put this in with the ground meat. Spice the mass of meat.

5. Part the ground meat into tablespoon-sized portions, press them flat, and lay some diced egg cubes in the middle of each portion. Press together the ground meat around this filling to form small balls.

6. Poach these balls (in desired amounts, portion-wise), for twenty minutes in the simmering Salsa-verde broth until they are soft. In the meantime, stir the meatballs often, then uncover them again. Serve on a dressed plate with the rest of the cilantro leaves sprinkled over the meatballs.

GRINGAS
DOUBLE-DECKER TORTILLAS
This dish is really easy to make and is very hearty and filling.

PRODUCES 4 SERVINGS
8 wheat flour tortillas
⅓ pound (150 g) middle-aged Gouda cheese
⅓ pound (150 g) Feta cheese
1¾ cups (400 g) Arrachera (page 85) (or Carnitas, page 129, Tinga de pollo, page 126, Verduras asadas, page 93)
2 tablespoons vegetable oil

WHEN SERVING:
crème fraîche
guacamole (page 51) and/or salsa of choice

PREPARATION
1. Heat the oven to 350°F (180°C).

2. Lay out four tortillas next to each other. Finely grate the cheese or crumble it, combine the cheeses and sprinkle this over the tortillas.

3. Dress your desired topping on top of the cheese and lay this on top of the extra tortillas.

4. Lightly oil a grill pan, brown the gringas in it for about two minutes, then carefully flip them and brown them again.

5. Divide the gringas into fourths and serve immediately with crème fraîche, guacamole, and/or your salsa of choice.

TACOS
FILLED CORNMEAL TORTILLAS

The filling for these tacos can be prepared several days in advance. You should enjoy these tacos immediately after preparation, since they simply taste the best this way.

PRODUCES 4 SERVINGS

12 small cornmeal tortillas
1¼ cups (300 g) Cochinita pibil
(page 130), alternatively, 1¼ cups
Barbacoa de pollo (page 90)
½ cup (120 g) Cebollas encurtidas
(page 109)

PREPARATION

1. Warm up the tacos in the oven.

2. Then lay them onto four large plates. Coat with Cochinita pibil or Barbacoa de pollo and Cebollas encurtidas.

3. Serve immediately.

ENCHILADA DE POLLO CON MOLE POBLANO
ENCHILADAS WITH A CHICKEN FILLING AND MOLE POBLANO

Chilies and chocolate are associated with Mexican cuisine, and rightfully so. The finely spiced and tangy dark chocolate seasoned sauce is a flavorful companion to many dishes.

PRODUCES 4 SERVINGS

1 pound (500 g) chicken breast
2 tablespoons vegetable oil
⅞ cup (200 ml) Mole poblano (page 95)
⅞ cup (200 ml) chicken broth
1 shallot
¼ cup (60 g) crème fraîche
8 tortillas
1 onion
salt

WHEN SERVING:
Mole poblano (page 95)
crème fraîche
Feta

PREPARATION

1. Heat the oven to 350°F (180°C). Rinse off the chicken breast with cold water, leave it to fully dry, and cover it with one tablespoon vegetable oil, then salt. Wrap it tight with aluminum foil and let it cook through for twenty to twenty-five minutes in the oven. Unwrap it from the foil and let it cool for a bit.

2. Heat the Mole poblano with the chicken broth in a pot and simmer for about five to ten minutes until it thickens somewhat.

3. Peel the shallot and finely chop it. Finely pick apart the meat. Warm this all up in a pot with the crème fraîche. Salt to taste.

4. Heat the extra vegetable oil in a pan and quickly flip the tortillas over in the pan until they become somewhat crispy. Peel the onion and cut it into paper-thin rings.

5. Using tablespoon portions, spread the Mole poblano over the tortillas. Finely pick apart the chicken meat and spread over the tortillas, then roll them up. Serve with Mole poblano, crème fraîche, and crumbled Feta.

ENCHILADA CON SALSA VERDE
ENCHILADAS WITH SALSA VERDE (*Tomatillo-Cilantro Salsa*)

This recipe for enchiladas with a freshly prepared salsa verde originates from the western part of the Mexican inland.

PRODUCES 4 SERVINGS

1 pound (500 g) chicken breast
1 tablespoon vegetable oil
salt
1²/₃ cups (400 ml) salsa verde (page 54)
1 shallot
²/₃ cup (160 g) crème fraîche
1 tablespoon vegetable oil
8 tortillas
¼ pound (100 g) Feta

WHEN SERVING:
Salpicón (page 108)

PREPARATION

1. Preheat the oven to 350°F (180°C). Shower the chicken breast with cold water, let it fully dry, rub on the vegetable oil, and salt. Tightly wrap it in aluminum foil. Let the breast cook through in the oven for twenty minutes. Unwrap it from the aluminum foil and let it cool down somewhat.

2. Heat the salsa verde in a medium-sized pot and let it reduce on very low heat for fifteen minutes.

3. Peel the shallot and finely chop it. Finely pick apart the meat. Warm both of these up with ¼ of a cup of crème fraîche in a small pot, then salt.

4. Heat the vegetable oil in a pan and quickly flip the tortillas over in the pan until they are somewhat crispy. Then flip them over in the salsa, fill them with chicken meat, and roll them up.

5. Fill the rolled tortillas in a casserole dish with the creased side facing downward and brush them with salsa verde. Cover the dish with aluminum foil and let them bake in the oven for ten minutes.

6. Crumble the Feta and serve with the rest of the crème fraîche on top of the enchiladas.

CHILAQUILES CON SALSA ROJA
TORTILLAS WITH SALSA ROJA (*Tomato-Chili Salsa*)

For this dish, you should use tortillas that are a bit old and stale, because they are the best at absorbing the salsa. A perfect use of leftovers!

PRODUCES 4 SERVINGS

12 stale corn tortillas (4½–6 in. or 12–15 cm)
2 cups (500 ml) salsa roja (page 56)
1¾ oz (50 g) middle-aged Gouda
1¾ oz (50 g) Feta
⅞ cup (200 g) Arrachera (page 85) (alternatively, Carnitas, page 129, or Tinga de pollo, page 126)

WHEN SERVING:
crème fraîche

PREPARATION

1. Divide the tortillas into eighths.

2. Warm up the salsa roja in a large, deep pan. Put the tortillas in the pan and fry them for five to seven minutes while stirring frequently until they have absorbed a lot of the liquid.

3. Grate the cheese or crumble it. Transfer the tortillas into a flat casserole dish, coat them as desired with Arrachera or another filling, and then sprinkle cheese on top of them. Gratinate shortly, then serve with the crème fraîche.

SCOTT'S TIP:
With two fried eggs on top, these tortillas transform into a filling breakfast.

CORDONIZ EN SALSA DE PÉTALOS DE ROSAS
QUAILS WITH ROSE PETALS

If you love Mexico, then you might like the book or film production of *Like Water for Chocolate* by Mexican best-selling author Laura Esquivel, a naturally bittersweet love story (see page 19), on which this recipe is based.

PRODUCES 4 SERVINGS

8 kitchen-ready quails
36 almonds
1 tablespoon beetroot juice
16 natural rose petals (red or pink)
1 garlic clove
1 teaspoon crushed Anise seeds
2 tablespoons butter
2 tablespoons honey
a few drops of rose water
salt and freshly ground black pepper

PREPARATION

1. Preheat the oven to 450°F (230°C). Wash the quails and dry them with a paper towel. Salt and pepper the inside and outside. Fold the wings under and tie the legs together with kitchen yarn. Lay the quails next to each other in an oven-tight form and cook them for ten minutes. Then reduce the oven temperature to 375°F (190°C) and cook them for another few minutes until they are soft. Then stab a fork into one quail leg. The leaking cooked juice should not be entirely pale pink. Keep them warm by covering them with aluminum foil.

2. For the sauce, roast the almonds for a few minutes in the oven until they turn golden-brown. Leave them to cool and finely grind them. Put the beetroot juice together with twelve rose petals and puree them.

3. Peel the garlic and finely chop it. Crush the Anise seeds. Melt the butter in a small pan then fry the garlic and Anise seeds in it for four minutes until golden-brown.

4. Stir the almond mix into the garlic butter and let them infuse while stirring often for ten minutes until the flavors combine. Then stir in the honey and the rosewater and spice the sauce as desired.

5. Press the sauce through a very fine sieve with a wooden spoon and spread it over the quails.

6. Arrange the quails onto places and serve garnished with the sauce.

TAMALES
FILLED CORN HUSKS

The preparation of tamales is a supreme discipline that takes up a lot of time. In Mexico, this dish is best prepared in a large round because although the recipe itself does not seem complicated, one can get caught on the intensity of the filling and wrapping. Because tamales belong to the most ordered dishes at Milagros, we have revealed our secret recipe to you. The filling has to rest for at least thirty minutes before it is rolled into the tamales. These tamales last for several hours when kept at room temperature in cling wrap.

PRODUCES 4 SERVINGS

1–2 garlic cloves
1 can of corn (1¼ cups or 300 g)
1²/₃ cups (400 ml) chicken broth
1 Serrano chili pepper
½ cup (120 g) cold lard
7 tablespoons (100 g) room-temperature butter
1 teaspoon baking powder
1²/₃ cups (400 g) Masa harina (cornmeal)
10 corn husks (page 31)
Tinga di pollo (page 126)
salt

PREPARATION

1. Brown the garlic clove(s) with the shell while turning them over for five minutes in a cast-iron skillet, then peel the shell. Let the corn grains drain and dry well and brown them in a pan while turning them over for five minutes.

2. Pour the chicken broth into the pan and warm it up somewhat. Wearing kitchen gloves, finely chop the Serrano chili peppers.

3. Puree the garlic, chili, and half of the corn grains with the broth until the corn grains are reduced to very small pieces, but still have somewhat of their structure.

4. Combine the lard, the butter, and the baking powder in a bowl, then beat thoroughly so that air is worked into the mix.

5. Work in the Masa Harina, beat for three minutes, then salt. First, stir in the corn broth, then add in the rest of the corn grains.

6. Wrap the filling in kitchen foil and let it rest for thirty minutes at room temperature until the liquid is fully absorbed. Then follow the basic instructions for tamales (page 31).

TINGA DE POLLO
CHICKEN WITH TANGY TOMATO SAUCE

This dish is very diverse; one can serve it as a main dish or use it also as a taco topping or filling in a burrito.

PRODUCES 4 SERVINGS

4 small chicken breasts
2 garlic cloves
1 onion
2 tablespoons vegetable oil
4 aromatic, ripe tomatoes
some fresh mint leaves
1–2 tablespoons pickled Chipotle chili peppers (Chipotle en adobo)
1 pinch of oregano
1 tablespoon white wine vinegar
salt

PREPARATION

1. Place the meat with one of the garlic cloves and half of the onions (both with their shells) in a pot and coat with water. Let them well up once, then cook them well on low heat for twenty minutes. Finely pick apart the meat and measure out about three tablespoons the poached broth.

2. Peel and finely chop the extra garlic clove and the extra half of the onions. Heat up the oil in a pan. Stew both in the pan on low heat until they are glazed.

3. Remove the stalks from the tomatoes, wash them, and chop them. Wash the mint and shake it dry. Thoroughly mix the tomatoes, mint, and Chipotle chili en adobo with the oregano and the chicken broth in a food processor, then put this through a sieve in the pan with the onion and garlic pieces.

4. Combine everything together well, salt, and warm it all up with the white wine vinegar for ten minutes. Stir in the meat and let it simmer for another few minutes until the stock becomes firmer.

CARNITAS
AROMATIC PORK

Germans are not the only ones that love pork; Mexicans love it too. In Milagros, it is served well-seasoned. The Coke is a secret tip, which gives it color and intensifies the flavor.

PRODUCES 6–8 SERVINGS

2¹/₃ pounds (1¼ kg) pork knuckle
1 pound (500 g) not-too-lean spare ribs
4 garlic cloves
1 natural orange
½ pound (250 g) smoked bacon
3 bay leaves
1 can of cola (1½ cups/350 ml)
1 tablespoon salt and freshly ground black pepper

PREPARATION

1. Rinse off the meat and dry it with a paper towel. Then debone the meat and cut it into about 3-inch (8 cm) sized cubes. Rinse off the spare ribs as well and dry them with a paper towel.

2. Peel the garlic cloves. Wash the orange and wipe it dry. Squeeze out the juice and peel the skin into strips.

3. Put all of the ingredients except for the coke into a stew/crock pot or Dutch oven with 1¾ quarts (1¾ L) water and let them well up once. Pour in the coke and stir everything thoroughly.

4. Let the meat stew for about one and three-fourths hours on very low heat until you can only see about ¾ inch (2 cm) liquid left in the pot. Remove the orange peel and the bay leaves.

5. Scrape the stew out from the bottom with a wooden spoon. Pick apart the meat into bite-sized pieces. Let everything simmer further while thoroughly stirring everything together until the poached water evaporates.

 SCOTT'S TIP:
Wrap the meat in tortillas (see picture) and arrange them on plates. Coarsely chopped cilantro, limes, or tomato salsa go really well with this dish.

COCHINITA PIBIL
BRAISED PORK

The main feature of this Yucatán Peninsula dish: it is marinated in a lot of citrus acids and the Mexican Epazote (Mexican tea root) spice comes together here. If you still are not familiar with Epazote, be careful with your dose; like with cilantro, its flavor is not for everyone.

PRODUCES 6–8 SERVINGS

⅓ cup (80 g) salt
⅓ cup (80 g) sugar
2¾ pounds (1¼ kg) pork loin with some fat
5 allspice grains
10 peppercorns
½ cup (125 g) Annatto paste (also known as Achiote paste)
½ cup (100 ml) bitter orange juice (alternatively, orange and grapefruit juice plus some squirts of lime juice)
1–2 garlic cloves
½ teaspoon oregano
½ teaspoon cumin seeds
4 banana leaves
1 small bunch fresh Epazote
2¾ oz (80 g) smoked bacon, finely sliced
salt and freshly ground black pepper

SCOTT'S TIP:
This recipe is very versatile. You can serve it easily on corn tortillas as a taco like in our picture, or you can use it as a filling in burritos, tortillas, or quesadillas.

PREPARATION

1. Prepare a brine from 2 quarts (2 L) cold water, salt, and sugar and put the meat in the brine. Crush the allspice grains and peppercorns and stir them into the brine. Cool the meat while uncovered for twelve hours or ideally overnight. Then lift the meat out of the brine, rinse it off, and dry it with a paper towel. Do not use the rest of the brine.

2. Stir the Annatto paste in with the bitter orange juice until the paste has the consistency of a thickened cream.

3. Let the garlic clove(s) brown in the shell in a cast-iron skillet for a few minutes. First, let it cool down, then peel.

4. Warm up the oregano and the cumin seeds in a pan until their aromas are released. Crush or grind the garlic clove(s) with salt and pepper and together with the oregano and cumin seeds, stir these in with the Annatto paste.

5. Preheat the oven to 375°F (or 190°C). Wash the banana leaves, dry them with a paper towel, and lay them on a baking sheet. Wash the Epazote and shake it dry.

6. Spread the meat onto the banana leaves and coat this with the marinade. Arrange the Epazote and the smoked bacon slices over this.

7. Lay the leaves over the meat so that it is fully covered and therefore cannot dry out. Slide the baking sheet into the oven and place an oven-safe pot filled with water next to the sheet. Cook the meat for about one and a half hours until it is butter soft.

JEWELS OF THE SEA
Fish and Seafood

A BASIC RECIPE FOR CEVICHE

The basic idea is always the same. Fish and seafood are marinated in citrus acids and then flavored as desired. Ceviche is a beloved snack in the entire South American region until almost Miami: refreshing, finely curbs your hunger, healthy, and very multi-variant.

PRODUCES 4 SERVINGS

30 kitchen-ready prawns
4 limes
½ cup (100 ml) olive oil
1 cup (250 ml) Mexican salsa
(page 53)
salt

PREPARATION

1. Wash the prawns and dry them. Lay these in a bowl and douse them with hot water. Let them stand for five minutes until they turn a pink color.

2. Drain the poached stock. Squeeze out the limes and soak the prawns consistently in the lime juice and lightly salt them. Let them infuse for fifteen minutes at room temperature.

3. Stir in the olive oil. Cover with kitchen foil and let them infuse for sixty minutes in the refrigerator. Stir in the Mexican salsa and spread the ceviche on individual plates or in small bowls.

SCOTT'S TIP:
Ceviche goes really well with tortilla chips. The finely aromatic fluid lends itself to be scooped up with a spoon, and the contrast between the crispy chips and delicate seafood is great!

CEVICHE DE MERO
HALIBUT CEVICHE WITH OLIVES

Raw fish, marinated only in lemon juice can have an intense flavor when paired with olives.

PRODUCES 4 SERVINGS

¾ pound (400 g) Halibut filet
3 limes
½ of a red onion
1 small tomato
1 Serrano chili pepper
10 green olives (i.e., filled with pimientos)
1 bunch cilantro
2 juicy oranges
salt

WHEN SERVING:
1 ripe, aromatic avocado

PREPARATION

1. Cut the Halibut filet into fine cubes and squeeze out the limes. Mix the fish and lime stock in a bowl and let this cool for sixty minutes while covered.

2. Peel the onion and finely chop it. Remove the stalks from the tomato, wash it, and finely chop it. Wearing kitchen gloves, halve the chili lengthwise, remove the seeds, and finely chop the pulp. Finely chop the olives. Wash the cilantro, shake it dry, and finely chop the leaves.

3. Drain the lime stock. Squeeze out the oranges. Together with the aromas and some salt, fold in the orange juice with the fish. Stir well and let this cool for at least four hours while covered.

4. Arrange the ceviche on small plates or in glasses when serving. Shell an avocado, finely dice it, or cut it into slices and garnish this on top of the ceviche.

CEVICHE DE PULPO
SQUID CEVICHE

For this recipe, fresh squid suits the dish especially well, and you can get it kitchen-prepared from your local fish monger.

PRODUCES 4 SERVINGS

1 pound (500 g) kitchen-ready squid
10 limes
3 ripe, medium-sized tomatoes
1 large red onion
1 ripe, aromatic avocado
1 bunch cilantro
1 bunch smooth parsley
2 Jalapeño chili peppers
¼ cup (60 ml) extra virgin olive oil
salt and freshly ground black pepper

PREPARATION

1. Simmer the squid in a pot with boiling water for twenty minutes, then rinse it off under cold water and divide it into fine, bite-sized pieces.

2. Squeeze out the limes, fill an appropriate-sized bowl with the squid, bathe it with the lime juice, and let it cool for twelve hours.

3. Measure out three tablespoons lime stock and drain the rest of it. Wash the tomatoes and remove the stalks, then peel the onion and shell the avocado. Finely dice the tomatoes and the avocado and finely chop the onion. Wash the cilantro and the parsley, shake them dry, and finely chop the leaves. Wearing kitchen gloves, halve the Jalapeño chili peppers lengthwise, remove the seeds, and finely chop the pulp.

4. Mix everything together well with the oil, salt, and pepper, and serve chilled.

TEQUILA PRAWNS

Good tequila comes in many degrees of maturity. The middle-aged Reposado, which we use in our restaurant for this recipe, has to mature for at least two years in an oak barrel.

PRODUCES 4 SERVINGS

1 natural orange
1 shallot
1–2 garlic cloves
16 kitchen-ready, cooked prawns
7 tablespoons (100 g) butter
2 Serrano chili peppers
1 small bunch cilantro
¼ cup of tequila (ideally Reposado)
sea salt

WHEN SERVING:
steamed or pan-fried rice

PREPARATION

1. Grate the orange peel into sheer zests. Scrape off the rest of the white inner skin with a hot spoon, if desired. Blanche the zests in boiling water and then rinse them under cold water. Repeat this process three times. Dry the zests with a paper towel afterward.

2. Peel the shallot and finely dice it. Peel the garlic clove(s) and finely chop it/them. Wash the prawns with cold water and let them dry.

3. Melt the butter in a pan on medium heat. Stew the shallot until it is glazed. Then cook the garlic pieces and the prawns in the onion butter on low heat while stirring frequently until the prawns turn a different color and curl up.

4. Wearing kitchen gloves, finely chop the Serrano chili peppers. According to your desired spice level, as mentioned earlier, halve the peppers lengthwise and remove the seeds and the white membrane. Wash the cilantro, shake it dry, and finely chop it.

5. Stir in the chili pieces and orange peel strips with the prawns. Then pour in the tequila and light it with a long match. Let the alcohol burn off. Now, stir in the cilantro and salt everything.

FISH WITH CRAB IN A RED SAUCE

This recipe combines white fish with our German crabs–delicious and very simple. You only have to plan for the two-hour marinating time, but this dish actually cooks itself.

PRODUCES 4 SERVINGS
½ pound (250 g) white fish filet
(i.e., golden redfish or red snapper)
3 limes
1 shallot
1 small garlic clove
½ pound (250 g) pulled crab
1 small bunch cilantro
1 ripe, aromatic avocado
1 cup (250 ml) ketchup
1 tablespoon pickled Chipotle chili
peppers (Chipotle en adobo)
salt and freshly ground black pepper

WHEN SERVING:
tortilla chips

PREPARATION

1. Lay the fish in a flat bowl.

2. Squeeze out the limes and sprinkle the juice over the fish. Chill the fish for two hours while covered and let it marinate.

3. Peel the shallot and the garlic clove and finely chop it or grate it. Fold the crab, the shallots, and the garlic into the marinated fish, then salt and pepper. Let this cool for thirty minutes while covered.

4. Wash the cilantro, shake it dry, and finely chop the leaves. Shell the avocado, remove the pit, and finely cut the pulp into fine strips.

5. When serving, pour the excess lime juice over the dish. Divide the fish into bite-sized pieces. Stir in the cilantro, the ketchup, and the Chipotle chilies and combine everything together well. Serve the ceviche in glass containers with slices of avocado.

CEVICHE DE VIEIRA
SCALLOP CEVICHE
For ceviche, all the ingredients must always be of top-fresh quality.

1 pound (500 g) kitchen-ready
scallops
4 limes
3 ripe, aromatic avocados
1 aromatic tomato
1 handful of cilantro leaves
1 Serrano chili pepper
^{1}/$_3$ cup (80 ml) extra virgin olive oil
sea salt

WHEN SERVING:
tortilla chips

PREPARATION

1. If needed, remove the scallops from the coral, wash them, then carefully dry them with a paper towel. Halve them lengthwise and lay them in a flat mold.

2. Squeeze out the limes and pour the juice over the scallops. Let them marinate for fifteen minutes at room temperature.

3. Halve the avocados and remove the pit. With a melon ball cutter, cut out the pulp into ball form.

4. Remove the stalks from the tomato, wash it, and dice it. Wash the cilantro, shake it dry, and finely chop the leaves. Wearing kitchen gloves, finely chop the Serrano chili peppers.

5. Drain the lime stock. Mix the scallops with the rest of the ingredients except for the avocado balls and arrange the scallop mix onto a plate. Spread the avocado balls over the scallops and serve immediately.

🌶 SCOTT'S TIP:
When marinating, use a clear glass container because then you can see if all of the ingredients are sitting in the lime juice.

CAMARÓNES AL COCO
COCONUT COVERED PRAWNS

A beautiful beginner recipe for prawns. Thanks to the sweetness of the coconut and the cornflakes, even kids will venture to try this dish.

PRODUCES 4 SERVINGS

12 kitchen-ready, cooked king prawns with unpeeled tails
1 small lemon
1/3 cup (80 g) flour
1 egg
½ cup (100 ml) milk
2 tablespoons (30 g) cornflakes
½ cup (100 g) coconut flakes
vegetable oil for frying
salt

PREPARATION

1. Put the king prawns in a bowl and coat them with cold water. Squeeze out the lemon and add the juice to the bowl. Soak the prawns in the juice for one minute, then lift them out of the water and carefully dry them with a paper towel.

2. Beat the flour, the egg, and the milk for the coating of the prawns and carefully salt this mixture. Mix the cornflakes and coconut flakes together and put this mixture onto a flat plate. Lay out a cooling rack and place baking parchment on it. Grip the prawns by the tail and first immerse them in the flour mix, then toss them in the cornflake-coconut mix. Let them rest on the cooling rack for several minutes until the coating becomes firm; then the coating should not fall off when frying the prawns.

3. Heat up the vegetable oil in an appropriate-sized pot to 350°F (180°C). Fry the prawns in serving-sized portions for one minute in hot oil and turn them over once in the frying oil. Then let the prawns dry on a paper towel.

 SCOTT'S TIP:
This dish tastes delicious with the American varieties of German apple sauce. They are somewhat more runny and work well as a dip.

TACOS DE MARISCOS EMPANICADOS
SEAFOOD TACOS

Fish tacos are surfer food and, admittedly, exist not only in Mexico. Do not be afraid of this long list of ingredients.

PRODUCES 4 SERVINGS

1 lime
1 teaspoon pickled Chipotle chili peppers (Chipotle en adobo)
½ of a garlic clove
1 teaspoon mustard powder
1 cup (250 ml) mayonnaise
3 allspice grains
10 cilantro seeds
½ of a bay leaf
1 pinch per ingredient: sweet ground paprika, cinnamon, cardamom, ginger
1 clove
1 pinch of cayenne pepper
½ teaspoon celery salt
1 cup (250 ml) butter milk
½ pound (200 g) white fish filet (i.e. tilapia)
½ pound (200 g) kitchen-ready squid rings
²/₃ cup (150 g) flour
vegetable oil for frying
freshly ground white pepper

WHEN SERVING:
salpicón (page 108)
12 small cornmeal tortillas
1 ripe, aromatic avocado
limes

PREPARATION

1. For the mayonnaise, squeeze out the lime and mix the juice with the Chipotle chili pepper in a bowl. Peel the garlic clove and finely chop it, then mix this in with the mustard powder, white pepper, and mayonnaise.

2. Grind the allspice grains and cilantro seeds in a mortar, finely crumble the bay leaf, and mix this in with the rest of the spices in a small bowl.

3. Fill up a bowl with the buttermilk and flavor it with one teaspoon of the spice mix. Cut the white fix filet in strips and put them with the shrimp and the squid rings in the buttermilk, then combine these together well.

4. Fill a re-sealable medium-sized plastic bag with the flour. In portions, shake the fish and seafood in the flour well so that they all are consistently floured. Put this aside.

5. In portions, heat up the oil in a large, cast-iron skillet and likewise add in portion-sized servings of the fish pieces and seafood in the pan, then brown these for four minutes.

6. When serving, spread the tortillas with the fish and seafood and arrange some mayonnaise and salpicón over this. Shell the avocado, remove the pit, cut the pulp into slices and layer them over the tortillas. Divide the limes into eights and serve them with the tortillas.

 SCOTT'S TIP:
The spice mix should be placed in an airtight container to retain its flavor and lasts for a few months.

PAPAYA-AVOCADO PRAWN SALAD

This salad is absolutely suitable for beginners, and also looks really impressive. This is exquisite as an elegant appetizer.

PRODUCES 4 SERVINGS

2 ripe avocados
1 small, ripe papaya
1 red bell pepper
½ pound (250 g) kitchen-ready, cooked prawns
¼ cup (60 g) unsalted sunflower seeds
2–3 tablespoons Vinagre de Milagros (page 63)
1 lettuce head

When garnishing:
aromatic, ripe strawberries
finely sliced red onions

PREPARATION

1. Shell the avocados and the papaya and finely dice them. Wash the bell pepper, halve it, clean it, then cut it into fine strips. Combine everything with the prawns, the sunflower seeds, and the vinaigrette in a bowl.

2. Clean the lettuce head, wash it, and spread the leaves onto four plates. Dress the prawn salad with dressing over the lettuce.

3. Wash the strawberries and halve them. Together with the onion rings, garnish the berries and rings on top of the salad.

SCOTT'S TIP:
Crab also works really well in this recipe.

TUNA FISH IN A CHILI-GINGER MARINADE

This quickly grilled tuna fish—which tastes best when cooked on a charcoal grill—has a really delicate flavor when combined with mango salsa (page 52) and rice.

PRODUCES 4 SERVINGS

4 slices of tuna fish amounting to ½ pound (200 g), about ¾–1 inch (2–3 cm) thick
2 dried Arból chili peppers
½ small red onion
1–1 ½ inches (3-4 cm) fresh ginger
1–3 cloves
1–2 limes
⁷⁄₈ cup (200 ml) soy sauce
¼ cup (50 g) sesame seeds

PREPARATION

1. Lay the tuna fish on an appropriate-sized baking dish.

2. Crumble the Arból chili peppers. Peel the red onion and finely chop it. Shell the ginger and finely chop it, grate it, or squeeze it. Crush the clove(s). Squeeze out the limes and mix the juice in with the soy sauce. Then stir in the rest of the aromas.

3. Fold the marinade in with the tuna fish. Marinate the fish for thirty minutes and turn it over once.

4. Lift the tuna fish out of the marinade and grill each piece 6 inches (15 cm) away from each other on the grill for four minutes on both sides.

LUBINA VERACRUZANA
SEA BASS VERACRUZANA

Veracruzana is a specific way to prepare fish with tomatoes, olives, and capers, similar to what we know of the Spanish kitchen. The Veracruz city lies on the Caribbean Coast of Mexico in the eastern part of the country. Jalapeño chili peppers were also originally cultivated there.

PRODUCES 4 SERVINGS

2¼ pounds (1 kg) sea bass filet (or white fish, as desired)
1 lime
1 onion
2 small garlic cloves
⅓ cup (80 ml) extra virgin olive oil
1¾ pounds (800 g) ripe tomatoes
2 small bay leaves
½ teaspoon oregano
10 green-stained olives
2 tablespoons capers
2 Jalapeño chili peppers
sea salt

PREPARATION

1. Prick the fish filet consistently with a fork. Squeeze out the lime, lay the fish in an oven-safe mold, and sprinkle the lime juice over the fish. Let the fish marinate for two hours while chilled.

2. In the meantime, peel the onion and the garlic cloves and cut them into paper-thin slices. Heat up a pan with two tablespoons olive oil. Sauté the onions and garlic in the olive oil on low heat until they are glazed. Remove the stalks from the tomatoes, wash them, chop them, and add them to the pan. Stir in the bay leaves and the oregano. Halve the olives and stir them together with the capers. Wearing kitchen gloves, halve the Jalapeño chili peppers lengthwise, remove the seeds, finely chop them, and stir these into the sauce as well. Salt the sauce and let it simmer for ten minutes.

3. Meanwhile, preheat the oven to 325°F (170°C). Spoon the sauce over the fish, then drizzle the rest of the olive oil over the fish. Loosely cover the fish with aluminum foil and cook it for twenty minutes. Douse the fish now and then repeatedly with the sauce.

MEXICAN KISSES

Desserts and Sweets

CHOCOLATE MEXICANO
AUTHENTIC MEXICAN HOT CHOCOLATE

Mexicans love it sweet, as you will see in this chapter. The only exception, of all things, is chocolate! Try this hot chocolate out, and I guarantee you will soon become nutty over this flavor mix, which has a waft of spice to it.

PRODUCES 1 QUART (1 L)

3 cups (750 ml) whole milk
1 cup (250 g) cream
1 level teaspoon cornstarch
½ pound (250 g) bittersweet chocolate
a few drops of vanilla extract
1 pinch of allspice powder
1 pinch of cayenne pepper
1 tablespoon honey or sweetener of your choice

PREPARATION

1. Warm up the whole milk together with the cream in a pot until the liquid forms small, light bubbles at the edges. Whisk two tablespoons of the milk-cream mix together with the cornstarch and stir this with an eggbeater until the mass thickens somewhat. Be careful when stirring so that the mass does not become too hot, otherwise it can burn easily.

2. Coarsely chop the bittersweet chocolate and stir this into the hot milk mix. Stir in the vanilla extract, the allspice, the cayenne pepper, and the honey. Beat the milk further with the egg beater until the chocolate has fully dissolved and a light foam has formed on the surface.

3. Spice as desired and serve hot.

CHURROS
SPRITZ COOKIES

This substantial dessert is beloved in the Spanish as well as the Mexican kitchen.

PRODUCES 12 PIECES

½ cup (120 g) sugar
1 pinch of cinnamon
½ cup (one stick/120 g) butter
1–2 tablespoons brown sugar
½ teaspoon vanilla extract
²/₃ cup (150 g) flour
5 eggs
1 quart (1 L) vegetable oil for frying
salt

PREPARATION

1. Mix the sugar and the cinnamon together on a plate.

2. Boil the butter, the brown sugar, some salt, and the vanilla extract with 1 cup (250 ml) water in a pot.

3. First, carefully fold in the flour with the blended butter mix with a hand mixer and then quickly work in the flour until it forms a dough ball. Pull the pot immediately from the stove.

4. Carefully stir the eggs in thoroughly, one by one.

5. Heat up the vegetable oil in a deep fryer or in an appropriate-sized pot. Either measure the temperature with a sugar thermometer (it should reach 360°F/182°C), or plunge the handle end of a wooden spoon into the pre-heated oil. If bubbles form around the handle, the oil is hot enough to start frying.

6. In serving-sized portions, fill the dough in a piping bag with a jagged, medium-sized nozzle. Push out three to four strips, each about 6 inches (15 cm) long, from the piping bag into the hot oil. Turn them after two minutes, then they will be somewhat browned. If they are too light in color, they will quickly turn soft when removing them from the pot.

7. Immediately toss the fried churros into the cinnamon-sugar mix and serve hot.

COCADAS
MEXICAN COCONUT MACAROONS

It is impossible to imagine the huge markets without fresh coconuts, to which Mexicans still go daily. They are a wonderful refreshment, especially in the summer when the temperatures become tropical. Shake the coconut before you buy it: if you do not hear any water, it is probably old or spoiled. Also, a shell without cracks and dry "eyes" (these are the dots) is an indication of freshness.

PRODUCES 12 PIECES

1 large coconut (for about 1⅔ cups/400 g of freshly grated coconut pulp)
4 tablespoons flour
1 pinch of baking powder
⅔ cup (150 g) sugar
5 egg whites
5 drops of almond extract
5 oz (150 g) bittersweet chocolate
salt

PREPARATION

1. Preheat the oven to 325°F (170°C). Bake the coconut for ten minutes in the oven, then take it out. Puncture the "eyes" with a screwdriver and drain the water. Wrap the coconut in a kitchen towel and tap it consistently on the outside with a hammer so that the outside shell breaks. Separate the pulp from the shell and grate it or shred it.

2. Lay out a baking sheet with baking parchment. Spread the coconut zest onto the parchment and roast it for about ten minutes in the oven until it turns a soft brown color. Take the sheet out from the oven and let it cool down. Do not shut off the oven.

3. Mix the flour and the baking powder together thoroughly. Carefully beat the sugar, the flour, and one pinch of salt with the egg whites. Then stir in the almond extract and the coconut zest.

4. With two spoons, measure out individual scoops from the mass and lay this onto the parchment of the baking sheet. Alternatively, fill up a piping bag with a broad, round nozzle, and form balls on the sheet from the mass. Increase the oven temperature to 350 °F (180°C). Bake the macaroons for thirty minutes until they are golden-brown, then let them cool down.

5. For the glaze, chop the bittersweet chocolate and melt this in a water bath. Plunge the cooled cocadas in the chocolate glaze and let the glaze turn solid on some parchment paper.

 SCOTT'S TIP:
If Mexico is the land of chocolate fans—most Mexicans like cocadas when they are freshly baked and eat them without the chocolate coating.

MELINDRES
MEXICAN MARZIPAN

Like with the Alpine Christmas bakeries, these little morsels are made with some lard. The lard creates a very fine, tender consistency. Start the day with the preparation before you start baking. These morsels should be kept in a cool and dry place in an airtight container, and they can last up to three weeks.

PRODUCES 15 PIECES

⅔ cup (150 g) almonds
⅓ cup (80 g) powdered sugar
2–3 tablespoons lard, without greaves
4–5 drops of almond extract
1 cup (250 g) flour
3 eggs
1 quart (1 L) vegetable oil for frying
1 cup (250 g) sugar
1–2 star anises, as desired

PREPARATION

1. Blanche the almonds and peel the skin. Let them dry somewhat. Then work them in with the powdered sugar in a mixer until it becomes an almond puree. Then transfer this into a food processor.

2. Now, work in the lard and the almond extract until it forms a smooth mass. Dust the flour into the mix and carefully stir this in until crumbs form. Separate one egg. Put aside the egg white. Stir the egg yolk and the rest of the eggs in with the mass. Beat this for another thirty seconds until it forms a dough. Measure out teaspoon-sized balls from the dough, roll them into a sphere, and work them into thumb-sized cookies; make a small indent into the dough balls by pressing into the center of the balls with your index finger. Put aside the rolled balls.

3. Heat the vegetable oil in an appropriate-sized pot until it almost reaches a smoking point. In serving-sized portions, fry the balls until they are golden-yellow, and roll them back and forth in the fat. Watch them constantly because thanks to the sugar content, these balls can easily burn. Let the finished fried balls dry on a paper towel.

4. Warm up the sugar and the star anises with one cup (250 ml) water and stir them until the sugar dissolves. Beat the egg white until it becomes stiff.

5. Extract the star anises as soon as the sugar syrup (at 240°F/115°C) becomes thick and gooey. Let the syrup flow in one thin stream into the egg white and beat this for one minute until a creamy, smooth, shiny mass forms.

6. Now, work quickly: from all sides, roll the balls through the sugar mass, then dry them on baking parchment and let them become firm.

YEMITAS
FIESTA PASTRIES

This pastry, which is given away at fiestas in Mexico (for example, birthday parties, weddings, and other celebrations or holidays), should be stored in an airtight container in the refrigerator and can last up to two weeks. Before serving, toss them again quickly in some powdered sugar.

PRODUCES ABOUT 36 PIECES

6 egg yolks
½ cup (100 g) sugar
1 natural lemon
1¼ cups (300 g) powdered sugar
2 tablespoons (30 ml) condensed milk (as desired)

PREPARATION

1. Warm up the egg yolks with the sugar in a water bath. Beat this with a hand mixer on the highest setting until the mass thickens in the steadily warm water bath.

2. Beat the mass further until it dissolves through the bottom of the water bath. This takes about ten to twelve minutes. Remove the mass from the stove.

3. Grate the skin of the lemon and stir this into the mass. Let the mass cool down somewhat.

4. Dust ⅞ of a cup (200 g) powdered sugar over the mass and stir this in until a dough forms. Knead the dough with your hands until it is no longer sticky and the sugar is fully worked into the dough. If the dough becomes too firm, pour in some condensed milk and work this into the dough.

5. Halve the dough and roll them both into about 1-inch (2 cm) thick rolls. Cut the rolls into finger-length pieces and form them into balls. The dough may form cracks with air pockets, but this can be easily solved by kneading it smoothly together again.

6. Scatter the rest of the powdered sugar onto a piece of foil and roll the finished balls into the sugar. Fill them into praline molds and let them dry out in the open for at least five hours or, ideally, overnight.

 SCOTT'S TIP:
Do not freeze the egg whites. They can be used for many different things, for example, mango mousse (page 162).

CAJETA
CARAMEL CREME

Try this dessert with goat's milk—unusual, but delicious! For the preparation, you will need a sugar thermometer. Cajeta lasts for several days when chilled in the refrigerator.

PRODUCES ABOUT 1½ CUPS (350 ML)

1 quart (1 L) goat's milk
1 cup (220 g) sugar
½ teaspoon vanilla extract
1 pinch of baking soda

PREPARATION

1. Heat the milk and the sugar with the vanilla extract in a large pot (at least 3 quarts/3 L, preferably copper). Stir regularly until the milk begins to simmer.

2. Pull the pot off the stove and stir in the baking soda. The milk triples in volume immediately (hence the large pot) and forms foam. First, place the pot on the stove again if no more bubbles are forming.

3. Warm up the milk again until it almost reaches a boiling point. Now, stir regularly until the milk reaches a light-brown color and is reminiscent of coffee. This can take up to an hour.

4. Measure the temperature with a sugar thermometer. As soon as the mass has reached 230°F (111°C), it will thicken. Now, you must constantly stir it so that it does not burn. Maintain the mass under its boiling point until it has reached 240°F (116°C), after about fifteen minutes. Now, the mass should be dark-brown and thickened, and it should remind you of the consistency of chocolate pudding.

5. Let it cool down, and this will further thicken the cream. Stir in hot water in spoonfuls if the cream has become too solid. Warm it up again if it is too runny.

6. Chill as desired. Before serving, bring the cream to room temperature.

CHOCOLATE CRÊPES WITH CAJETA

You can freeze the batter in addition to the finished, baked crêpes.

PRODUCES ABOUT 15 CRÊPES

3 eggs
¾ cup (180 ml) milk
²/₃ cup (150 g) flour
2 tablespoons sugar
½ teaspoon vanilla extract
1½ tablespoons orange liqueur
(i.e., Cointreau)
⁷/₈ cup (700 g) cream
10 beautiful, aromatic strawberries
3 tablespoons butter
salt

Chocolate salsa

4 oz (120 g) bittersweet chocolate
¼ cup (60 g) cream
1 teaspoon cinnamon powder
1 tablespoon sugar

WHEN SERVING:
Cajeta (page 160)

PREPARATION

1. Mix the eggs, milk, and a ½ cup (100 ml) water with the flour, sugar, vanilla extract, and the orange liqueur with a mixer. Let the batter rest in the refrigerator for one hour until it is smooth and there are no more bubbles to be seen.

2. In the meantime, beat the cream with one pinch of salt until it is stiff. Remove the stems from the strawberries, wash them, carefully dry them on a paper towel, and cut them into fine slices.

3. In serving-sized portions, heat up the butter in a cast-iron skillet. Fry up the batter in spoonfuls to form a paper-thin sized portion by spreading the batter back and forth consistently on the pan. Turn the crêpe over after thirty seconds. Fry it for another ten seconds, then take it out of the pan and put it aside. Repeat this process with the rest of the batter.

4. For the salsa, coarsely chop the chocolate. Slowly heat up the cream in a water bath and stir it smoothly. Add in the cinnamon powder, transfer this to a serving bowl, and sprinkle it with sugar.

5. When serving, spread the warm crêpes by alternating with the chocolate salsa and the cajeta, roll them up, and serve them garnished with cream and strawberry slices.

SCOTT'S TIP:

If you still want to give the salsa another kick, season the crêpes with some coffee liqueur. Measure out about two tablespoons and stir the liqueur (i.e., Kahlúa) together with the cinnamon powder in the melted chocolate.

MANGO MOUSSE

In Mexico, fresh mangos are used in this recipe, of course. In Germany, it is not always easy to find ripe, aromatic mangos, for which we have developed a recipe from our restaurant, which also works well with mango puree from the can or with frozen goods.

PRODUCES 4 SERVINGS
3 tablespoons sugar
1 cup (250 g) cream
2 eggs
3 egg whites
3 limes
1 cup (250 g) mango puree
(canned or frozen, defrosted)

WHEN SERVING:
beautiful strawberries

PREPARATION

1. Let the sugar melt in a small, cast-iron skillet on very low heat until it caramelizes. Then put this aside.

2. Beat the cream with the eggs and the egg whites with a blender until this becomes frothy. Mix in the caramelized sugar with the mango puree.

3. Squeeze the limes by either dividing them into thirds lengthwise and then squeezing them with your hands, or use a special lime press to squeeze them. Mix the juice in with the sugared mango puree. Blend in the cream mix with the puree in a bowl.

4. Fill some cocktail or wine glasses up with the mouse. Serve them garnished with strawberries.

FLAN DE CHOCOLATE Y KAHLÚA
CHOCOLATE FLAN WITH COFFEE LIQUEUR

Prepare this dessert one day in advance because it tastes better when it has time to cool through. This is also ideal for when you have guests, since you will want to have the least amount of stress possible when entertaining them.

PRODUCES 6 SERVINGS

½ cup (100 g) fine sugar
²⁄₃ cup (150 g) brown sugar
1 cinnamon stick
1 cup (250 ml) condensed milk
1 cup (250 g) cream
2 oz (60 g) bittersweet chocolate
3 tablespoons Kahlúa liqueur
½ cup (125 ml) milk
1 cup of strongly brewed espresso
3 eggs
2 yolks

WHEN SERVING:
strawberries, Physalis or Cape gooseberries, or currants

PREPARATION

1. Draw up a small pot with the fine sugar, ½ cup (100 g) brown sugar, cinnamon stick, and three tablespoons water and let them simmer for fifteen minutes while stirring constantly until the sugar is dissolved and the liquid has taken on a caramelized consistency.

2. Distribute the liquid into six flan molds; smooth out the bottoms and tops. Preheat the oven to 350°F (170°C).

3. Warm up the condensed milk with three tablespoons cream in a small pot. Chop the bittersweet chocolate and stir this in with the condensed milk until it is melted. Add in the Kahlúa-Coffee liqueur.

4. In another pot, mix the milk together with the rest of the cream, the espresso, and the rest of the brown sugar. Slowly heat this up until small bubbles form on the edges of the pot.

5. Mix in all of the eggs with the egg whites. Pull the milk off of the stove and in spoonfuls, beat this in with the eggs. When everything is work in, bring this mass back and pour it into the pot, then firmly beat this mixture again (otherwise they will become scrambled eggs). Then work in the chocolate-Kahlúa liquid and take this off the stove immediately afterwards.

6. Spread the mass onto the flan molds. Bake these in a water bath in the oven for sixty minutes. The flans should really then be solid. Let the flans cool down at room temperature and chill them overnight.

7. When wobbly, hold down the edges of the molds alongside with a sharp knife until the masses become a bit more relaxed. Plop these onto individual plates and as desired, serve them garnished with strawberries, Cape gooseberries, or currants.

INDEX

♨ SCOTT'S SHOPPING TIPS

It is a lot of fun to try out a foreign cuisine if the ingredients are authentic. I have put together a list of typical Mexican ingredients for you (see below) that we use very often in our restaurant, and you can refer to the addresses mentioned below for these ingredients.

Chili peppers can be fresh, dried, and pickled in oil or brine. For example, Chipotle and Jalapeño chili peppers are often canned. **Hominy** is dried corn with which polenta is prepared (does not sound too tasty, but it is). Also, **Annatto paste** (Achiote paste) and the seeds can be found in the shops listed on page 173, and the same goes for canned **rose water** or **mango puree**. Do not forget about **bean puree**, which a lot of Europeans associate with Mexican cuisine.

In our restaurant, we do not make our own **tortillas** anymore; that would really be too elaborate. We can buy them directly in stores or on the Internet. As you have probably already noticed, if you have already flipped through the book, we flavor our dishes with typical Mexican-style, largely diverse selection of chili peppers.

You can find a lot of ingredients that we use in the typical Mexican kitchen in stock at your local Asian food store. Fresh **mangos**, **avocados**, or **chili peppers**, which one can freeze excellently, fresh **banana leaves** for wrapping (which also freeze excellently), **hibiscus petals** or **tamarind paste** should be available there. Also, you can strike it rich in the freezer aisle, for example, you can find prepared, kitchen-ready mango puree for our desserts. You can of course bring **dried herbs** or **chilies** back from your next (or first) vacation to Mexico.

Since I am a huge tequila fan and want to instill this in you as well, I am giving you my favorite addresses on the Internet. On "123 Tequila," you can get **tequilas** made from 100 percent Agave, which beats the lines at the supermarket.

123 TEQUILA
www.123tequila.de
email: info@123tequila.de

PACIFIC ONLINE SPIRITS
www.pacificonlinespirits.com
email: sales@pacificonlinespirits.com

THANK YOU

For me, it was a matter very close to my heart to build the restaurant Milagros and to make our customers aware of authentic Mexican cuisine. And from my heart, with all due respect, there are some people who have made this endeavor even more meaningful.

First, I would like to thank my wife, Heike, and our three wonderful children, Charlotte, Isabella, and Lukas, from the bottom of my heart. Their support and consolation are my foundation, on which I can always lean.

My wonderful designer, Heather Barker from Roam Studio deserves a huge special thanks; she designed the look of the restaurant and perfectly captured the Mexican beauty within it; as well as her husband, Florian Carl, whose support and advice for the concept and the execution of Milagros were extremely important.

Most recipes in this book were developed in combination with an absolute connoisseur of the Yucatán kitchen, Chef David Sterling, who runs the culinary school, *Los Dos*, in the gorgeous colonial city of Mérida. David Sterling teaches and shares his wisdom with the persuasiveness of a preacher. His contribution will always be a part of the Milagros history.

I cannot forget—this is obvious—my restaurant team. One is only as good as one's people, with whom one surrounds oneself, and I am so lucky to be surrounded by so many gifted and devoted people, who have worked very hard so that Milagros would become a success. I would like to thank my head chef, Richie Wee, who accompanied me in Mexico and in whom I have confided my trust with the place of history and techniques of authentic Mexican cuisine in the finest details, and upon which he built and led the best Mexican kitchen in all of Germany after his return. I would also like to thank my Mexican cooks, who decided to emigrate and move to Germany in order to share their kitchen secrets with others—a very special thanks to the extremely gifted and super-nice Jorge Omar Aguilar Palomino, and the same goes to Omar Reyna Alvarez. Also, I would like to thank "Mr. Salsa," a.k.a. Terry Caddik, who makes the best salsas in the European mainland on a daily basis.

I am as proud of my service team as I am of my kitchen team. Their suffering for the marketing of Milagros and their commitment to our guests quintessentially embodies the Mexican tradition of *Mi casa es tu casa*. Thank you all, Ninja, Andrés, Bianca, Tobi, Susana, and all the others in the service team, for what you achieve for Milagros.

All successful business owners need a person who can work with any kind of theme in any kind of situation. For me, this person is my manager, Kristina Ganghofer. Thank you, Kristina, for being there from the beginning and for sticking it out by operating the unending labyrinth of the regulations in Germany.

The Milagros family is a proud supporter of a wonderful relief organization for children, who call themselves "Nuestros Pequenos Hermanos" (NPH). For fifty years, NPH has cared for abandoned and orphaned children from Mexico and other South American countries, as well as the Caribbean. NPH provides these children with food, clothing, and shelter, and in addition, they provide them with an education and with medical support. NPH is an affectionate surrogate family for over 17,000 children. For this reason, Milagros is donating 100 percent of this cookbook's profits to NPH. More information can be found on *www.hilfefuerwaisenkinder.de*.

The history of Mexican cuisine is very closely tied to tradition and family—especially to mothers and grandmothers, who have, with their hard work, provided for their families for many centuries, and who, at the same time, have burst forth with a cuisine, which truly has earned its place among the best in the world. I would like to dedicate to these warm-hearted, bold, and talented women and their spirit this special note of thanks:

Gracias a ustedes y nuestra protectora, La Virgencita, por todo que se han sacrificado para la famila y por todo que se han contribuido a nuestra felicidad!

Scott Myers

First published in 2012 under the title *Rezepte Aus Mexiko* by Neuer Umschau Buchverlag GmbH, Moltkestrasse 14, 67433 Neustadt/Weinstrasse, Germany.

Skyhorse Publishing books may be purchased in bulk at special discounts for sales promotion, corporate gifts, fund-raising, or educational purposes. Special editions can also be created to specifications. For details, contact the Special Sales Department, Skyhorse Publishing, 307 West 36th Street, 11th Floor, New York, NY 10018 or info@skyhorsepublishing.com.

Skyhorse® and Skyhorse Publishing® are registered trademarks of Skyhorse Publishing, Inc.®, a Delaware corporation.

Visit our website at www.skyhorsepublishing.com.

10 9 8 7 6 5 4 3 2 1

Library of Congress Cataloging-in-Publication Data is available on file.

ISBN: 978-1-62873-758-5

Printed in China